STOCK MARKET INVESTING

OYENIKE ADETOYE

©2023 by Oyenike Adetoye.

This book is designed to highlight a comprehensive journey through the fundamentals of investing. **'Stock Market Investing: From The Ground Up!**' unravels stock market investment strategies, serving as a guide for beginners and a refresher for seasoned investors

This book is sold with the understanding that neither the author nor the publisher is engaged in rendering legal, accounting, or other professional services.

Each situation is unique, and questions relevant to personal finances should be addressed to an appropriate professional to ensure careful and appropriate evaluation.

The author and publisher expressly disclaim any liability, loss, or risk incurred as a consequence, directly or indirectly, of the use and application of the contents of this work.

While all stories and anecdotes described in the book are based on true experiences, most names are pseudonyms, and some situations and characteristics have been slightly changed for educational purposes and to protect individuals' privacy.

OTHER BOOKS BY OYENIKE ADETOYE

- NonSecrets of the Financially Secure – Volume 1

- NonSecrets of the Financially Secure – Volume 2

- NonSecrets of the Financially Secure – Volume 3

- NonSecrets of the Financially Secure – Volume 4

- NonSecrets of the Financially Secure – Volume 5

- Praying for your Finances

- Financial Nakedness

- Financially Smart Teens & Young Adults

- The Beauty of Compounding

- The Four Letter Word D E B T

- Financial Boundaries

- Finances Biblical Affirmation

- Financial Success Quenchers

- The Irrefutable Laws of Money

- Stock Market Investing

DEDICATION

This book is dedicated to my wonderful readers.

Thank you for embarking on this writing journey with me ♡

ACKNOWLEDGEMENTS

To God, who inspired the writing of this book.

To my darling husband and beautiful daughters, whose unwavering support illuminated even the late nights and early mornings spent penning this work.

To my amazing siblings, whose strength and encouragement fortified me throughout this journey.

To everyone who has supported my dreams and inspired me to keep writing.

Thank you so much!

Oyenike.

Contents

"How many millionaires do you know who have become wealthy by investing in savings accounts? I rest my case." — Robert G. Allen.

READING THIS BOOK

Thank you for reading this book. In the pages that follow, you will discover the wisdom of seasoned investors, explore real-world case studies, and gain practical insights that can be applied to your own investment journey. **"Stock Market Investing: From The Ground Up!"** provides you with the foundational knowledge and key strategies needed as an individual investor to navigate the stock market.

The stock market is an arena of infinite possibilities, where dedication and knowledge can transform your financial future. My goal is to unpack the thousands of resources out there into one comprehensive playbook. Consider this your essential hand-held guide to stock market investing basics, best practices, and mistakes to avoid. Whether you are just getting started or looking to improve, this book will help you gain the confidence to invest in stocks the smart way.

I have grouped this book into sections for ease of reading. **Part 1** is all about making sense of investing. It discusses the simple definition of investing and how our mindsets shape our money decisions. This section also explores the key differences between saving and investing, debunks myths and false beliefs about investing, and outlines the catalysts of successful investing.

Part 2 delves into the definition of the stock market. We will deep-dive into the evolution of the stock market and provide a step-by-step overview of how it works. This section concludes by discussing the essential information needed to be adequately prepared for the awesome journey of investing.

In the **3rd part**, we embark on the journey into stock market investing by discussing the rules of investing, what to invest in, when to invest, and how to invest. The section concludes by exploring risks, returns, and the distinguishing features of a good or bad stock.

Part 4 of this book focuses on the different types of financial instruments. From shares to bonds, and other derivatives like Options and futures, this chapter explores the varieties of investment vehicles, providing insights into the pros and cons of each.

Part 5 deep-dives into investment portfolio management. Opening a brokerage account, creating an investing portfolio, and tracking and evaluating investment performances are covered here. This section concludes by discussing investing costs and fees.

Part 6 delves into smart investment strategies, and **Part 7** explores various investment choices available to us as we delve into the intricacies of building a well-rounded investment portfolio.

The last two sections of this book (**Part 8 and 9**) are dedicated to fully exploring how to handle emotions while investing, the pitfalls and mistakes we must avoid, and investment illustrations that shows the steps to follow when opening investment accounts with brokerage companies.

By the time you finish this investing resource, complex market terms like share prices, dividends, mutual funds, and index funds will all make sense. You will feel prepared to profitably invest your hard-earned money, transforming the stock market from confusion to opportunity. So, let's get started.

The journey this book will take you on begins with understanding why investing matters in the first place. Learning the core principles of stocks and the broader market will allow you to maximize returns and steadily build future wealth over time. Turn the page, and let's dive into the fascinating world of investing together. The journey towards financial freedom through stock investing starts here!

INTRODUCTION

In a world driven by economic growth and financial prosperity, the stock market stands as a dynamic arena where fortunes are made, dreams are shattered, and wealth is multiplied. It is a place where investors have the opportunity to carve their path to financial success, and yet, it can be a labyrinth of complexities for the uninitiated.

Welcome to **"Stock Market Investing: From The Ground Up!",** a book designed to be your trusted companion on the journey to financial empowerment. Whether you are a seasoned investor, a novice just stepping into the world of stocks, or someone looking to refine their investment strategy, this book is your essential roadmap to navigate the intricacies of the stock market with confidence and acumen.

In these pages, we will embark on an enlightening exploration of the stock market, covering its history, its function in the global economy, and the fundamental principles that underpin successful investing in the stock market. This book is not merely about chasing quick riches; it's about developing a sustainable and well-informed approach to creating and preserving wealth through stocks and shares.

By the end of this book journey, you will possess the tools to make informed decisions, seize opportunities, and navigate market turbulence with resilience. "**Stock Market Investing: From The Ground Up!**" is not a promise of overnight riches but a promise of knowledge and wisdom to fortify your financial future.

In case you are wondering who I am to be offering you advice about your personal finances; I am a qualified Chartered Management Accountant professional who has experienced fiscal highs and lows, been in and out of debt, and has worked in various multinational FTSE 100 companies in the United Kingdom for several years. I founded LifTED Financial Consulting Ltd as a result of my personal discoveries and experiences with money on my journey to financial freedom.

So, are you ready to embark on this transformative journey of investing? Let us unlock the doors to prosperity together and begin our exploration of the fascinating world of stock market investing one page at a time. Welcome aboard!

---------Disclaimers---------

I am not a CPA, attorney, insurance, or financial advisor, and the information in this book shall not be construed as tax, legal, insurance, or financial advice. If you need such advice, please contact a qualified CPA, attorney, insurance agent, or financial advisor.

Neither the author, the publisher, nor anyone involved in the production of this book has a financial stake in any financial product mentioned in the book. Nor does anyone receive any kind of compensation from any of the products or companies mentioned.

PART 1:

INVESTING PHILOSOPHY AND MINDSET

1. What Is Investing?

Investing can be defined as the process of putting your money to work for you. It involves using your money to buy an asset you believe has a good probability of generating a safe and acceptable rate of return over time.

When done properly, investing can make more money for you than the interest you might earn in a savings account. However, with reward comes risk. If an investment is executed incorrectly and you make poor choices, you could lose your money.

An important lesson I have learned about personal finance and wealth-building is that you can accumulate wealth more quickly by putting your money to work daily, rather than just sending yourself to work every day. The true art of investing is all about allowing your money to work for you. It's about placing it into the right venture and letting it sit and grow over time.

You can't absorb all there is to know about investing in a single day, but thankfully, that is not a prerequisite to starting your journey as a successful and profitable investor. I strongly believe that anyone can reap substantial financial benefits from simply taking the time to learn the basics of investing.

If you don't invest, you are missing out on opportunities to increase your financial worth. Building lasting wealth and growing your money can only occur through investing.

In investing, risk and return are two sides of the same coin. Low risk generally means low expected returns, while higher returns are usually accompanied by higher risk. Even though investing might sound daunting, you will still be better off taking that leap of faith and getting started - your money can't grow otherwise. Not investing can cost you a lot more money than losing a little money on a bad investment.

The realm of investing offers an infinite number of things to learn. The most successful investors will tell you that they are continually learning and constantly refining and expanding their skills!

2. Saving Vs. Investing

The words 'saving' and 'investing' are sometimes used interchangeably, but there is a significant difference between the two. When it comes down to it, we should engage in both to secure our financial future. I often tell people that saving is the starting point of investing - you cannot be a good investor if you are not a good saver. Let's look at the definition of these two terms.

Saving is the simple act of setting money aside in a secure place where it remains until you need to access it. It might earn a little interest depending on where you put it, and it will be available for emergencies or to achieve your savings goals. Savings are liquid assets that can be accessed, utilized, and deployed immediately with minimal delay. Popular savings products include a savings account, a current or checking account, and a certificate of deposit.

Investing takes the concept of saving a step further. It is the process of putting your money to work for you by purchasing assets that you believe have a good probability of generating a safe and acceptable rate of return over time. When done correctly, investing can yield higher returns than the interest you might earn in a savings account. However, greater rewards also come with greater risks. If investments are made poorly or unwise choices are made, you could potentially lose your money.

Similarities Between Saving and Investing

i.   Money Accumulating Strategy:

Saving and investing both share a common goal – they are both strategies that help you accumulate money.

ii.   Future Benefits:

Saving and investing both involve putting money away for future reasons. When we analyze the rationale behind embarking on these financial strides, we discover that we deliberately put money away for the future.

iii.   Financial Planning:

Planning is an integral part of personal finance. Failing to plan ideally translates to planning to fail. The processes associated with either saving or investing involve the analysis and planning of what you want and how you will achieve your goals.

iv.   Risk Management:

Both activities involve some level of risk. While saving in traditional bank accounts is generally low-risk, it still involves the risk of inflation eroding the purchasing power of your money. Similarly, investing carries risks related to the performance of the assets you invest in.

v.   **Investing Is A Form Of Saving:**

The journey towards long-term investment begins with mastering the basics of saving. Experts argue that saving sets the blueprint or pedestal for investing. Think of savings as the building block of investment - the foundation upon which a financial house is built!

It is important to recognize that while they share these similarities, saving and investing serve different purposes within your financial strategy. Saving provides liquidity and safety for short-term needs while investing aims for higher returns and wealth accumulation over the long term. The key is to strike a balance between the two that aligns with your financial goals and risk tolerance.

Saving is the starting point of investing - you cannot be a good investor if you are not a good saver.

Differences Between Saving and Investing

i. ## Duration:

Saving is short-term oriented, typically under 5 years, while investing is long-term oriented, extending beyond 5 years. The duration is based on the specifics of the goal.

ii. ## Risk:

A key difference between saving and investing lies in the magnitude of risk. Saving money has little risk of loss but offers minimal gains. When you invest, however, there is the potential for better long-term gains or rewards, along with the potential for loss.

iii. ## Interest:

The goal of investing is to generate more money, while the goal of saving is to keep money safe, thereby making very little or no return. Investing helps you beat inflation through the interest earned, ensuring that your money's purchasing power stays strong.

iv. ## Typical Products:

The best types of products for saved money include secure savings accounts from reputable banks, Certificates of Deposit (CDs), or money market accounts. With investing, typical products include pensions, stock market investments in shares and bonds, real estate investments, and alternative investments like gold and silver.

Saving is the starting point of investing. You can only invest if you cultivate the habit of saving. Once you've mobilised an adequate sum for meeting your emergencies, you're all set to begin your journey as an investor.

Experts argue that saving sets the blueprint or pedestal for investing. Think of savings as the building block of investment - the foundation upon which a financial house is built!

3. It All Starts With Your Money Mindset

Investing isn't merely about crunching numbers and analyzing data. It is equally, if not more, about the mindset you bring to the table. A strong and disciplined mindset is often the distinguishing factor between successful investors and those who struggle.

Your money mindset is your unique set of beliefs and your attitude about money. It drives the decisions you make about saving, investing, spending, and handling money. It shapes what you believe you can and cannot do with money, how much money you believe you're allowed, entitled, and able to earn, how much you can and should spend, the way you utilize debt, how much money you give away, and your ability to invest with confidence and success.

What you believe about money, yourself, and the world shapes how your life will unfold. What's fascinating about your money mindset is that this core set of beliefs resides in your unconscious mind. And it can hang out there, dormant. But, by becoming a keen observer of your thoughts, feelings, bodily reactions, and interactions with money, you gain awareness of your current set point and the ability to change or shift your mindset.

Many of our core beliefs about money are formed in early childhood by observing and internalizing the money messages we learn from our parents, friends, community, and other caregivers - especially our parents. Growing up, my mom only saved money. Her frequent advice that I should always save for rainy days still rings through my ears, even now that I am older. I never heard about investing from any of my circle of influences while growing up. So, I grew to only embrace saving my money, and oh, was I good at it!

I was an amazing saver. The comfort and satisfaction of witnessing my savings account balance increase month-on-month were truly gratifying. At that time, my knowledge of investing was limited. The most daunting aspect of my understanding of investing was the fear that I could lose my hard-earned money due to the inherent risks. Consequently, I opted to steer clear of investing and concentrated solely on saving my money.

The Shift

Understanding your money mindset and its origins is crucial for making positive shifts and changes. Transforming your money mindset begins with awareness. My perspective on investing began to change when I delved into more readings on the subject and tuned into podcasts that highlighted the benefits of investing rather than fixating solely on the associated risks.

Let me pause here and say this: as you become more aware of your mindset, you will encounter your own limiting beliefs and money blocks that impede the shift. This is perfectly normal; we all have money blocks. They never go away. Limiting beliefs and money blocks keep resurfacing in newer and different forms. Your task is to continually uncover these blocks, dissolve them, and release them so you can build a healthier and more confident relationship with your money.

After addressing my limiting beliefs and money blocks surrounding the fear of investing, my perspective began to change. It was a slow but steady transformation that liberated my way of thinking. I started to see investing as an opportunity to put my money where I knew it would yield more returns for me.

If you happen to be like the former me, who found comfort in only saving money, here is a bit of awareness for you. This realization highlights how much you might be missing out on if you solely save and don't invest. Shifting your money mindset begins with awareness.

4. Investing Myths

In the process of writing this book, I conducted extensive research to understand why people don't invest. I can personally relate to the excuses some individuals give, such as high-interest debt payments and the fear of losing money. However, I also discovered that other excuses were rooted in myths and misconceptions about investing or a lack of knowledge about the process.

Myths are faulty belief systems learned over time. They are simply not true and need to be debunked. Numerous myths related to investing circulate as truth, but, in reality, these myths hinder people from embracing the benefits of investing. I have compiled seven common investing myths below. It's about time we debunk these long-believed 'truths' for what they really are - MYTHS.

Myth 1: You Need A Lot of Money:

One of the most common myths about investing is the belief that you need a substantial amount of money to get started. This couldn't be further from the truth. If you can allocate £50 or $50 a month in your budget, you can and should start investing. If you think you can't squeeze that amount into your budget, consider adjusting your expenses or exploring income generating ideas to make it happen.

Now, if you carry high-interest debt or don't have emergency savings, you should attend to that first. But once you do, investing should be a priority on your list.

Myth 2: It's Too Risky To Invest:

Certainly, investing carries inherent risks, as indicated by the common warning that "you may not get back what you invest." However, this doesn't mean it's too risky to engage in. All investments fall along a risk spectrum. At one extreme end of the spectrum, there are high-risk investments—not for the faint-hearted. At the more sedate end of the spectrum, you will find some very low-risk investments. Regardless of your risk tolerance, there are investment options available to match your comfort level, ranging from the extremely cautious to the highly adventurous and everything in between.

Myth 3: Investing Is Too Complex:

When we don't understand something, it's human nature to consider it too complex for us to master, leading us to neglect it altogether. Faced with a new financial challenge, negative thoughts like "I'm not good with money" or "I'm not smart enough to invest" often surface. These are self-limiting beliefs that can be overcome by seeking more understanding. While the concept of investing may initially appear daunting, viewing your lack of knowledge as an opportunity for growth, rather than a lack of ability, can help break self-imposed barriers. As Warren Buffett succinctly puts it in one of his quotes: "Investing is simple, but not easy."

Myth 4: Investing Is Only for Rich People:

Perhaps in the past, investing was perceived as a pursuit reserved for the wealthy. Today, this is a myth! It has never been easier for anyone to invest, even with limited funds. Fractional shares have removed the entry barrier that once existed. People can now invest in stocks that used to cost thousands of pounds or dollars with just a few pounds or dollars. For example, as of the time of writing this book (October 2023), a single share of US stock Berkshire Hathaway is priced at $534,132. In the past, you would need substantial capital to invest in such a company. Thanks to the availability of fractional shares, you can now invest in expensive stocks without having to break the bank. You can simply invest the specific amount available in your budget.

Myth 5: The Stock Market Is the Only Investing Option:

When people think of investing, their minds often gravitate toward stocks and shares. However, there are other types of investments that offer diversification, such as bonds, real estate, commodities, and currencies. If the stock market makes you apprehensive, there are alternative investment choices to explore.

Myth 6: Investing Is Too Time-Consuming:

Some people envision an investor as someone who constantly studies financial reports and spends hours adjusting stock screeners to find the right stock at the perfect time. But you don't need to be watching price changes daily. And you certainly don't need to be buying, selling, or moving your money around in reaction to market fluctuations. Often, a hands-off investor ends up with more favourable results than a busy one. If you engage in index investing, you may not have to exert much effort to find the ideal fit. Robo-advisors can assist you in constructing a portfolio based on your long-term goals and risk tolerance, all without consuming more than a few minutes of your time.

Myth 7: Investing Is Just Like Gambling:

This is a common concern for many individuals. While there are some similarities, such as both involving risk and choice, specifically the risk of capital with the hope of future profit, there are important distinctions. Gambling is typically a short-lived activity, whereas investing can last a lifetime. Additionally, on average and over the long term, gamblers face a negative expected return, whereas investing typically carries a positive expected return over the long run – the odds are consistently in your favour.

I often ask people to tell me their 'WHY' for investing. It is essential to understand the motivation behind your decision to invest your money. It's perfectly acceptable to have multiple answers to this question, but it becomes problematic if you have no answer at all. Having clear reasons or purposes for investing is crucial for achieving success in your investing endeavours.

5. Catalysts Of Successful Investing

In the investing world, a catalyst is anything that precipitates a drastic change in the outcome of an investment. The three catalysts that positively affect the outcome of investments are: the power of compound interest, time, and patience.

1. <u>Compound Interest:</u>

Compound interest refers to the process by which your initial investment earns interest, and that interest then generates additional interest over time. It's like a cycle of earning 'interest on interest,' and it has the potential to exponentially increase your wealth. This is often referred to as your money working for you, and its impact can be remarkably powerful.

Albert Einstein famously referred to compound interest as the 'eighth wonder of the world.' Those who grasp its significance can harness this force to accelerate their wealth. Conversely, those who overlook it may find themselves struggling with mounting debts that seem to grow perpetually.

One fascinating aspect of compound interest is its universality. It does not discriminate. If you're cash-rich, compound interest can make you richer by growing your wealth when you invest. And if you're bad-debt poor, compound interest can make you poorer by also growing your debt. It has no respect for age, race, gender, ethnicity, or religion. Anyone in the world can benefit from compound interest, and its influence can be profound.

Let's look at a simple example of how compound interest works. Let's say you have £100 to invest, paying 7% interest each year for ten years. At the end of the first year, you'd have £107. Then in year two, you would get 7% of £107, which is £7.49, totalling £114.49. And at the end of ten years, you'd have £196.72. Not only does the amount you invested grow each year, but the interest gained from the previous year also grows. That's why it is called compound interest.

The power of compound interest is one of the best reasons to start investing early. Because you earn interest on your interest, once you set it in motion, it takes on a life of its own - even if you never add another penny to your principal. The longer your money remains invested, the greater the compounding effect.

The table below illustrates how compounding works. If someone invests £10,000 yearly and leaves the money invested in the stock market over a period of years assuming a conservative 5% annual return, more than

£100,000 profit would have accrued over 50 years of letting the money grow.

How Compounding Works

Time Invested	Amount	Return*	Total
1 year	£10,000	£500	£10,500
10 years	£10,000	£6,289	£16,289
20 years	£10,000	£16,533	£26,533
30 years	£10,000	£33,219	£43,219
40 years	£10,000	£60,400	£70,400
50 years	£10,000	£104,674	£114,674
60 years	£10,000	£176,792	£186,792

*Assumes 5% annual returns net of fees and charges

Understanding and harnessing the power of compound interest is a fundamental concept for achieving your financial goals and building wealth. Whether you are saving for retirement or other financial objectives, the sooner you start and the longer you let your money compound, the more significant the impact will be on your financial well-being.

2. Time

Compound interest and time are intertwined, with time being the most crucial factor in earning compound interest. The more time you have, the longer your money has to grow.

Success in investing comes from the time spent in the market, not from timing the market.

Consider the graph below. The first investor invested £50,000 and remained in the market for a 20-year period. The second investor put in exactly the same amount (£50,000) but only started investing 10 years later.

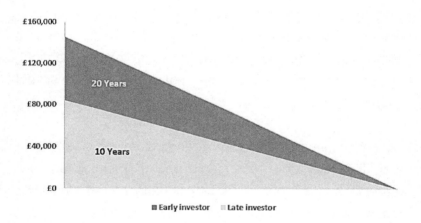

Investor	Invested Amount	Time Invested	Ending Balance
Early investor	£50,000	20 years	£145,408
Late investor	£50,000	10 years	£83,754

As seen in the graph, both investors initially invested the same amount (£50,000) at the same average return of 7%. The sole difference between these investors is the amount of time their money had to grow. The longer you have to invest and allow your returns to compound, the greater the potential for your investments to grow. This principle underscores the importance of starting early and maintaining a long-term perspective in your investment strategy. When it comes to investing, there is no substitute for time.

3. <u>Patience</u>

Patience is the third catalyst that makes investing work, working hand in hand with the other two catalysts - compound interest and time. It is crucial to understand that compound interest won't turn you into a millionaire overnight; building wealth requires time, patience, and consistent contributions.

Successful investors acquire a range of valuable skills over their lifetimes, and patience is one of them. We aren't naturally born patient, and a lack of patience is a significant reason why many people refrain from investing. However, patience can be learned and, if you are an investor, mastering it can propel you toward your financial goals.

Patience often entails remaining calm in situations where you lack immediate control. Being patient means enduring short-term challenges for the promise of future rewards. Impatient investors who let anxiety and emotions dictate their decisions can significantly harm their long-term returns. Wealth takes time to grow, and patience is the key to unlocking its potential.

This quote by Charlie Munger encapsulates the essence of patience in investing: "Waiting helps you as an investor and a lot of people just can't stand to wait. If you didn't get the deferred-gratification gene, you've got to work very hard to overcome that." - Charlie Munger.

Patience and investing are natural partners. Wealth takes time to grow, and patience is the key to unlocking its potential.

PART 2:
THE STOCK MARKET

6. What Is The Stock Market?

The stock market is a financial marketplace where buyers and sellers meet to trade shares, each representing a small ownership stake in a company listed on an exchange. In exchange for your cash, a business offers you a share in its future, making you a 'shareholder' with a tiny slice of ownership in that company.

Here are some key points to know about stock markets:

- They provide a centralized place for the trading of stocks and stock-based securities. The London Stock Exchange was the world's first stock market. Other well-known stock markets globally include the New York Stock Exchange (NYSE), NASDAQ, Hong Kong Exchanges, and the Saudi Stock Exchange, among others.

- Not all companies are publicly traded. Only those that choose to issue shares to the public through an initial public offering (IPO) are listed on stock exchanges and can be bought and sold by investors. To be publicly traded on stock exchanges, companies must meet regulatory requirements, demonstrating solvency and transparency, among other criteria.

- Companies issue shares of stock to raise capital for various purposes, such as expanding operations, funding research and development, or paying off debt. When individuals or institutions purchase these shares, they become partial owners of the company.

- Financial activities within a stock market are conducted through institutionalized formal exchanges or Over-The-Counter (OTC) marketplaces that operate under defined regulations. The stock market is one of the most vital components of a free-market economy, allowing companies to raise money by offering stock shares and corporate bonds.

- The stock market enables common investors to participate in the financial success of companies, earn profits through capital gains, and receive dividends, though losses are also possible. In the long term, the stock market fosters capital formation and economic growth for the country.

- Stock prices are influenced by the dynamics of supply and demand in the market and fluctuate throughout trading days. News, earnings reports, and analyst ratings all play a role in price changes. When more people want to buy a particular stock than sell it, the price tends to rise, and vice versa.

- Stock market indices, such as the S&P 500, Dow Jones Industrial Average, and NASDAQ Composite, are used to track the overall performance of the stock market or specific sectors. These indices provide a snapshot of how the stock market is doing on a given day.

- Investing in the stock market involves both opportunities for financial gain and the risk of losing money. Stock prices can be highly volatile, and various factors, such as company performance, economic conditions, and geopolitical events, can influence market movements.

- Over extended periods, the stock market tends to trend upward, reflecting economic growth and company profits. However, it also experiences volatility and risk. Many investors opt for a long-term perspective when investing in the stock market to build wealth over time.

The stock market serves as a barometer of economic health and is a central component of the financial system.

7. Evolution Of The Stock Market

The stock market, a cornerstone of modern finance, has a rich history that spans centuries. Its evolution reflects changes not only in financial systems but also the growth and transformation of economies worldwide.

Understanding the evolution of the stock market is essential for anyone seeking to navigate its complexities and comprehend its role in the global economy. Here is an overview of the stock market's evolution:

i.   Early Beginnings (17th Century):

The stock market's roots can be traced back to the Amsterdam Stock Exchange, established in 1602 by the Dutch East India Company. This marked the world's first official stock exchange, where shares of the company were traded among investors.

ii.   Birth Of Corporations (18th Century):

The 18th century saw the rise of joint-stock companies in various industries. As stock trading gained popularity, more formalized stock exchanges emerged, such as the London Stock Exchange, founded in 1801.

iii. Industrial Revolution And Expansion (19th Century):

The 19th century saw the Industrial Revolution transform economies. The stock market played a crucial role in financing new industries, railways, and infrastructure projects, leading to substantial economic growth.

iv. Global Expansion (20th Century):

The 20th century marked a period of global expansion for stock markets. There was increased regulation and investor protection measures. Exchanges were established in various countries, and innovations like electronic trading and stock indices (e.g., the Dow Jones Industrial Average) were introduced.

v. Technological Advancements (Late 20th Century):

The late 20th century witnessed a tremendous increase in globalization and technological advancements. The adoption of electronic trading in the late 20th century revolutionized the stock market, allowing for faster and more efficient trading, making it accessible to a broader range of investors.

vi.   **High-Frequency Trading And Online Brokerage (21st Century):**

The 21st century witnessed the rise of High-Frequency Trading (HFT), where computer algorithms execute trades in milliseconds. Additionally, online brokerage platforms made investing accessible to many. This has increased liquidity and efficiency but also introduced new challenges.

vii.   **Globalization And Interconnected Markets (21st Century):**

In the 21st century, stock markets have become more interconnected globally. Events in one market could impact others worldwide due to increased cross-border investments and interdependence.

viii.   **Digital Disruption, Modern Trends, and Innovation (21st Century):**

Beyond traditional stocks and bonds, alternative investments like cryptocurrencies and exchange-traded funds (ETFs) gained popularity, offering new opportunities and challenges for investors.

ix.   **Sustainability and ESG Investing (21st Century):**

The stock market has evolved to include a focus on environmental, social, and governance (ESG) factors.

Investors increasingly consider sustainability criteria when making investment decisions.

The evolution of the stock market mirrors the dynamic changes in the global economy, technology, and investor behaviour. As the financial world continues to evolve, the stock market will likely adapt to meet the changing needs and demands of investors and societies around the world.

Successful investing is not about timing the stock market perfectly; it's about making informed decisions, staying disciplined, and always learning.

8.   How The Stock Market Works

The stock market is a complex financial system that facilitates the buying and selling of ownership shares in publicly traded companies. It serves as a critical component of the global financial system, enabling companies to raise capital and investors to buy and sell securities. Below is a step-by-step overview of how the stock market works:

i.   <u>Companies Go Public:</u>

The stock market begins with companies deciding to "go public." This process involves a company offering a portion of its ownership, called shares or stocks, to the public for the first time through an Initial Public Offering (IPO). This process typically includes working with investment banks to underwrite the offering.

ii.   <u>Stock Exchanges:</u>

Stock exchanges are centralized marketplaces where the trading of shares occurs. These exchanges serve as intermediaries, facilitating the buying and selling of stocks. Prominent stock exchanges worldwide include the New York Stock Exchange (NYSE), NASDAQ, London Stock Exchange, and Tokyo Stock Exchange.

iii. Listing On An Exchange:

After an Initial Public Offering (IPO), the company's shares are listed on one or more stock exchanges. This means the shares can be publicly traded, and their prices determined by supply and demand in the market.

iv. Investors And Brokerage Accounts:

Individuals and institutions, such as mutual funds, pension funds, and hedge funds, can buy and sell stocks through brokerage accounts. They place buy or sell orders through brokers or online trading platforms. These orders can be market orders (executed immediately at the current market price), limit orders (executed at a specified price or better), or stop orders (executed when a stock reaches a specified price called a stop price).

v. Price Discovery:

The stock market operates based on the principles of supply and demand. When more people want to buy a stock than sell it, the price typically rises, and vice versa. News, earnings reports, and economic factors can influence stock prices.

vi. Settlement:

After a trade is executed, a settlement process occurs. It involves the exchange of cash and ownership of shares between the buyer and seller, typically taking a few days to complete.

vii. **Stock Indices:**

Stock indices, such as the S&P 500 or the Dow Jones Industrial Average, track the performance of a specific group of stocks. These indices are used as benchmarks to assess the overall health and direction of the stock market.

viii. **Market Volatility:**

Stock markets can be subject to fluctuations due to factors such as economic conditions, geopolitical events, corporate earnings reports, and investor sentiment. Volatility is a natural part of the market's dynamics.

The stock market is a dynamic and integral part of the global financial system, enabling companies to raise capital and investors to participate in wealth creation. While it can seem complex, understanding the fundamental workings of the stock market is essential for anyone looking to invest or engage with the financial world. Successful stock market participation often involves a combination of research, prudent decision-making, risk management, and a long-term perspective.

9. The Stock Market Can Go Down And Up

One of the first things new investors notice about the stock market is its constant fluctuation - some days prices are up, and other days they are down. These movements can seem erratic and unpredictable in the short term, but it is normal to see the market make significant swings up and down.

Major events, economic forces, company performance, investor psychology, and more can impact overall market sentiment, causing prices to rise and fall. No one can predict exactly when the market will go up or down on any given day or year.

However, historically over long periods of many decades, the general trend of the stock market is to increase in value. This reflects the growth and profits of companies over time. The market goes through periods of gains (Bull Market) as well as periodic downturns and corrections (Bear Market).

The stock market is known for its volatility, and the prices of stocks can fluctuate both upwards and downwards.

Reasons for Upward Movements (Bull Markets)

i.   Economic Growth:

Positive economic indicators, such as strong GDP growth, low unemployment rates, and rising consumer confidence, can drive investor optimism and lead to a bullish market sentiment.

ii.   Corporate Earnings:

Strong corporate earnings and revenue growth can boost stock prices. Investors often purchase stocks in anticipation of higher future profits.

iii.   Interest Rates:

Low or falling interest rates can make stocks more attractive compared to other investments like bonds or savings accounts. Lower borrowing costs can also benefit companies, increasing their profitability.

iv.   Market Sentiment:

Positive news, developments, or sentiment in the financial markets can lead to a surge in buying activity, pushing stock prices higher.

v. **<u>Innovation and Technological Advances:</u>**

Companies that innovate and adapt to changing consumer preferences and technological advancements tend to outperform, attracting investor interest.

<u>Reasons for Downward Movements (Bear Markets)</u>

i. **<u>Economic Downturns:</u>**

Economic recessions or contractions can result in reduced consumer spending, lower corporate profits, and pessimism in the market, leading to declining stock prices.

ii. **<u>Interest Rate Increases:</u>**

Rising interest rates can increase borrowing costs for companies and consumers, potentially impacting corporate profitability and slowing down economic growth.

iii. **<u>Geopolitical Events:</u>**

Events such as political instability, trade disputes, or conflicts can introduce uncertainty into the market, causing investors to sell off stocks in favour of safer assets.

iv.   **Market Corrections:**

Periodic market corrections, which are typically short-term declines of 10% or more from recent highs, can be triggered by various factors, including profit-taking and valuation concerns.

v.   **Earnings Disappointments:**

If companies report lower-than-expected earnings or provide negative guidance, it can lead to a sell-off of their stocks.

vi.   **Investor Sentiment:**

Negative sentiment, panic selling, or fear in the market can result in a cascade of selling, pushing stock prices lower.

It's important to note that market movements are often influenced by a combination of these and other factors. Additionally, stock markets do not move in a straight line but experience periods of both upward and downward trends over time. Investors should be aware of these fluctuations and carefully consider their investment goals, risk tolerance, and time horizon when participating in the stock market. Diversification, a long-term perspective, and a well-thought-out investment strategy can help individuals navigate the inherent volatility of the stock market.

Investors often face the risk of losing money when stock prices decline, but they also have the opportunity to profit when prices increase. This inherent uncertainty is a fundamental characteristic of the stock market, and it's important for investors to be aware of the potential for both gains and losses.

10. Preparing To Invest In The Stock Market

One of the best financial decisions you can make for yourself is to start investing. The good news is that you don't need to be a financial professional, have a Ph.D. in finance, or read the finance section of the newspapers to begin. Here are a few things you need to know to be adequately prepared before embarking on this exciting journey of investing in the stock market.

i.   <u>Educate Yourself:</u>

As Benjamin Franklin rightly put it: "An investment in knowledge pays the best interest." When it comes to investing, nothing will pay off more than educating yourself. Knowledge is an essential asset when you're investing; knowledge is power. The most important thing you can do to be a successful stock market investor is to learn, learn, and never stop learning.

Stock market investing isn't complicated if you are willing to spend the time learning about it. Read books on investing, listen to investing podcasts, attend seminars and workshops that discuss investing, keep an open mind, and ask questions of successful investors. Remember, you only know what you know; be willing to learn, unlearn, and relearn.

ii. <u>Have a Plan And Set Clear Financial Goals:</u>

Planning and setting goals are crucial when embarking on your stock market investing journey. During the planning stage, honestly answer questions like: How much budget can I allocate to investing monthly? How long will it take to reach my investing goal? How much risk can I take? What types of investments should I consider? Answering these questions may take some time, but the insights gained are invaluable for your planning.

iii. <u>What Is Your Reason For Investing:</u>

Understanding the motivation behind your decision to invest that spare cash is critical to stay 'committed to the cause' and to avoid straying off course in times of uncertainty. Determine why you want to invest. Are you investing for retirement, to leave a legacy, to take part in economic growth, to fund a major purchase, or to build wealth? There are many solid reasons to consider investing in the stock market. Determining your goals and motivations can help you decide if they align with your financial strategy.

iv. <u>Develop A Simple Investment Strategy:</u>

Decide whether you want to be a long-term investor or a more active trader. Your strategy should align with your goals and risk tolerance. The simpler your investment strategy, the better. Create a straightforward portfolio spread across two or three different asset classes and stick to it as a starting point. Complicated investment strategies often require much more work and stress than simpler ones do, often for no more profit. A simple investment approach prevents you from becoming overwhelmed and keeps you on track.

v. **Start Small, Keep Contributing, And Watch Your Money Grow:**

The reason many people don't invest is that they feel they don't have enough money to invest. There is a misconception that you need lots of money to become an investor, but nothing could be further from the truth, especially today. Lots of barriers to entry have been removed and you can start investing with as little as £10 or $10.

Don't be afraid to start small. Begin with sums of money that you can afford to lose and do not risk too much while learning. As you watch your balance grow, you will become more comfortable investing more considerable sums if you can afford to. Compound interest is the primary principle behind investing. More money in your account means more interest is compounded.

vi. <u>**Be Ready to Ride Out The Highs And The Lows:**</u>

More often than not, things don't always go as planned. Stocks are going to go up and down. Bonds are going to go up and down. Real estate is going to go up and down. Don't be discouraged. Always remember you are in this investing gig for the long haul.

Stock prices rise and fall, economies expand and contract, and investors with risky plans panic. Making a panicked move based on a short-term drop or a short-term jump is probably going to put you in a worse long-term position, especially when you add in transaction fees and taxes (if applicable). Start small, learn along the way, diversify your portfolio, and exercise lots and lots of patience. Patience is a virtue you need when investing!

vii. <u>**Consult With A Financial Advisor:**</u>

Asking for help is not a sign of weakness. If you ever reach a crossroads and don't know how to start with investing, consider seeking advice from a qualified financial advisor or planner. They can help you create a personalized investment strategy based on your goals, risk tolerance, and financial situation. A professional can also provide guidance and help you avoid costly mistakes.

Investing in the stock market can be a rewarding way to achieve your financial goals, but it requires careful planning and discipline. By following these steps and consistently educating yourself about the world of investing, you can embark on a journey to build wealth and secure your financial future. Remember, successful investing is not about timing the market but time in the market.

Investing in the stock market can be a rewarding way to achieve your financial goals, but it requires careful planning and discipline.

PART 3:

GETTING STARTED WITH STOCK MARKET INVESTING

---

11. Rules Of Investing

We can't start stock market investing without a thorough deep dive into the rules of investing. You shouldn't consider investing money if doing so means risking a roof over your head or defaulting on the payment of essential bills and other necessities.

I have highlighted a few golden rules you must know before venturing into investing. Make sure you seek professional investment advice for more clarity before you embark on your stock market investing journey.

Rule 1: Know Your Investment Goal

What is your 'WHY' for investing? What do you want to invest in? Are you investing for retirement, to earn an income, to pay for your children's education, or to grow your fortune? Having a clear purpose for investing and knowing exactly what to invest in is critical for investing successfully.

Rule 2: You Need Money To Invest

Investing is the act of allocating money with the expectation of generating income or profit. You need money to invest, so having an income is a must (preferably a steady income). It is recommended that one should consistently invest over time to enjoy the full benefit of compounding and the Dollar-Cost Averaging (DCA) strategy. We will discuss DCA in more detail in Chapter 26.

You shouldn't think about investing money if doing so means risking a roof over your head or defaulting on the payment of essential bills.

Rule 3: You Have A Solid Emergency Fund:

Smart investors must have an emergency fund in place to cover sudden unemployment or unforeseen emergencies. You must be able to weather a storm when life happens. Ideally, you should set aside 3 to 6 months of your basic living expenses before you start investing. This will help prevent the need to sell investments prematurely. The emergency fund takes priority over investing.

Rule 4: You Have Paid Off Your High-Interest Debt:

High-interest debts, such as credit card debt, can erode your finances faster than investment gains can build them. This is crucial because, in the long run, the money you'll be spending on interest payments for your high-interest debt is higher than any returns you will earn from your investments. It's generally advisable to pay off high-interest debt before investing. One works for you, and the other works against you. Focus on eliminating the one that could drag you down—your high-interest debts.

Rule 5: Don't Invest Money You'll Need Right Away:

Investing is for the long term, typically five years or more. Some investments require you to tie up money for months or even years to earn returns, and withdrawing early can trigger penalties. If you are going to need cash right away, such as for next month's mortgage or next year's university/college tuition, you don't want to risk not being able to access the money when you need it. A good rule of thumb is to keep cash in a savings account if you'll need it within the next two years, rather than investing it.

Rule 6: You've Done Your Due Diligence And Research:

Throwing your money haphazardly into investments you don't understand is a sure way to lose it quickly. Never invest in something you don't comprehend. Taking calculated risks requires understanding both the potential reward and the likelihood of loss. To avoid significant losses, take the time to research the fundamentals of what, where, and how you are investing your money.

Rule 7: Invest Early And Invest As Much As You Can:

One essential investing strategy is to start sooner and stay invested longer. This allows compounding to flex its muscles. Compound interest works its magic on your money, turning small and steady investments into a substantial nest egg that buys financial freedom. The sooner you start investing in assets that produce a reasonable rate of return, and the more you invest in those assets, the harder your money will work for you.

Rule 8: Know Your Risk Tolerance:

Understand your risk tolerance, which is your ability and willingness to endure fluctuations in the value of your investments. Your risk tolerance should guide your investment choices. How much risk can you tolerate? What will allow you to sleep at night? Are you an aggressive or conservative investor? Higher risk is associated with a greater probability of higher returns, and lower risk is associated with a probability of smaller returns.

Rule 9: Have Realistic Expectations On Performance:

Realistic expectations of how your investments will perform are crucial. For example, the average return of the stock market since inception (1801) has been 8%. This is an average, meaning you will not experience this every single year. In a bull market (a time when the price of stocks is rising), you could see returns of 20% per year or more. And in a bear market (a time when the price of stocks is falling), you could see a 20% loss or more. Despite the peaks and valleys, over the long term, an 8% return has remained consistent.

Are you an aggressive or conservative investor?

Rule 10: Diversify Your Portfolio:

Don't put all your eggs in one basket. Try to diversify as much as you can to lower your risk exposure. To reduce the likelihood of significant losses, spread your money across a mix of different asset classes. By diversifying across various industries (e.g., pharmaceuticals, technology) and different countries, you can protect yourself against the ups and downs of any one part of your portfolio.

Rule 11: Don't Miss Out On Employer's "Free Money":

In many employer-sponsored retirement plans, the employer will match some or all of your contributions. If your employer offers a retirement plan and you do not contribute enough to get your employer's maximum match, you are passing up "free money" for your retirement savings. Don't be one of those people who wait until their friends start retiring to begin investing. The sooner you start investing, the earlier retirement will become an option for you.

Rule 12: Keep Costs Low:

Investment costs are unrecoverable; every penny paid in management fees, taxes, transaction fees, and trading expenses is money out of your pocket. These costs do add up, compounding along with your investment returns. In other words, you don't just lose the tiny amount of fees you pay; you also forfeit all the growth that money might have had for years into the future. Costs are one of the driving factors that dictate whether you will reach your goal, and they are among the many factors completely within your control. So, give them the time and attention they deserve.

Rule 13: Don't Panic:

Investments can go down as well as up. Don't be tempted to sell funds just because everyone else is. Emotion is the enemy of smart investing. Do not let emotions like fear and anxiety cause you to make the rash decision to sell into a falling market. Many people want to invest and get quick cash, but thinking this way commonly leads to making wrong, poor investments.

To get the best returns from your investments, you must be prepared to think LONG-TERM.

12. Ways To Invest In The Stock Market

There are several ways to invest in the stock market, and the choice often depends on individual preferences, risk tolerance, and financial goals. Here are some common ways to invest in the stock market:

i. Individual Stocks:

Buying individual stocks means purchasing shares of a specific company. Stocks represent ownership in a company, and when you buy shares, you become a shareholder, owning a portion of that company. This means that when the company makes money, so do you. However, when the price of a company's stock goes down, the value of the owner's investment also goes down.

Investing in individual stocks typically requires a significant amount of time and effort for research. Successful individual stock investing involves understanding the companies you are investing in, analyzing financial statements, assessing industry trends, and staying informed about broader economic conditions. If you find yourself uncertain about managing this level of research, it may be prudent to explore alternative investment options.

ii. <u>Mutual Funds:</u>

Mutual funds are investment vehicles that pool money from multiple investors to invest in a diversified portfolio of stocks, bonds, or other assets and securities. Mutual funds are operated by professional money managers, who allocate the fund's assets and attempt to produce capital gains or income for the fund's investors after taking a fee.

Investing in a mutual fund is a good way to avoid some of the complicated decision-making involved in investing in individual stocks. Mutual funds offer diversified holdings which makes them very attractive. The cost of trading is spread over all mutual fund investors, thereby lowering the cost per individual.

iii. <u>Exchange-Traded Funds (ETFs):</u>

Exchange-Traded Funds (ETFs) are investment funds traded on stock exchanges, functioning as baskets of assets traded like securities. Combining features of mutual funds and individual stocks, ETFs offer investors a way to gain exposure to diversified portfolios encompassing assets like stocks, bonds, commodities, or a mix of classes.

Unlike mutual funds, ETFs can be bought and sold on an open exchange, providing more control over purchase prices and typically carrying lower fees. The diversification provided by ETFs helps spread risk across various securities, reducing the impact of poor performance by any single investment.

iv. **Index Funds:**

Index funds are a type of mutual fund or exchange-traded fund (ETF) designed to track the performance of a specific market index. Rather than relying on active management, which involves fund managers selecting individual securities, index funds aim to replicate the performance of a particular index (e.g., S&P 500 or FTSE 100).

They provide broad market exposure, diversifying investments across multiple stocks. Investors in index funds indirectly own shares of stock in numerous companies. These funds are passively managed, resulting in lower fees and overall costs.

v. **Dividend Stocks:**

Dividend stocks are shares of companies that distribute a portion of their profits to shareholders in the form of dividends. Typically paid out regularly - such as quarterly or annually - dividends provide investors with a steady income stream in addition to potential capital gains.

While dividend stocks can offer a reliable income stream, they come with risks. Stock prices may fluctuate, and companies might reduce or suspend dividend payments during challenging economic times. Building a dividend-focused investment portfolio requires diversification and thorough research.

vi.   **Stock Options / Options Trading:**

Stock options are financial instruments that give the holder the right, but not the obligation, to buy or sell a specific amount of a company's stock at a predetermined price within a specified time frame.

Options trading can be complex and involves a degree of risk. Despite the potential for high returns, especially for those well-versed in the mechanics of options, there is also a risk of significant loss. Investors should fully understand the complexities, assess their risk tolerance, and weigh potential rewards before engaging in options trading.

vii.   **Bonds:**

Bonds are debt securities that represent a loan made by an investor to a borrower, typically a government or corporation. When you buy a bond, you are essentially lending money to the issuer in exchange for periodic interest payments and the return of the principal amount at maturity.

Bonds are considered relatively safer investments compared to stocks because they offer a fixed interest rate and the return of the principal amount at maturity. We will deep-dive more into bonds in chapter 17.

viii.   Real Estate Investment Trusts (REITs):

Real Estate Investment Trusts (REITs) are investment vehicles that own, operate, or finance income-generating real estate across various property sectors. The primary purpose of REITs is to allow individuals to invest in large-scale, income-producing real estate without directly buying, managing, or financing properties.

REITs offer a way for investors to gain exposure to real estate as an asset class and earn a share of the income produced by those real estate investments. Like any investment, REITs come with their own set of risks. They are sensitive to changes in interest rates, economic conditions, and the real estate market.

ix.   Direct Investment Plans (DRIPs):

Direct Investment Plans, often referred to as DRIPs, are investment programs that allow investors to purchase shares of a company's stock directly from the company itself, bypassing traditional brokerage firms. DRIPs are typically offered by large, established companies as a means to promote long-term investment and foster shareholder loyalty.

While DRIPs offer benefits such as low costs and dividend reinvestment, they may also come with limitations or restrictions. Additionally, it's important to note that not all companies offer DRIPs, so investors interested in this approach should verify whether the companies they are interested in have such plans available.

x. **Commodities:**

Commodities are physical goods that are interchangeable with other goods of the same type and are typically traded on commodity exchanges. They can be broadly categorized into two types: hard commodities and soft commodities.

Examples of hard commodities include gold, silver, oil, natural gas, copper, etc. Investors can gain exposure to hard commodities through various means, including commodity futures contracts, commodity-focused ETFs (exchange-traded funds), and stocks specific to commodities.

Examples of soft commodities are agricultural products such as wheat, corn, soybeans, coffee, and cotton. Investors can access soft commodities through futures contracts, commodity ETFs, and stocks of companies involved in the production and distribution of these commodities.

Unlike stocks that may pay dividends, commodities generally do not generate income. Investors rely on price appreciation for returns. Including commodities in a diversified investment portfolio can provide a hedge against inflation and add diversification benefits, as commodity prices may not always move in tandem with traditional financial assets like stocks and bonds.

Before deciding on an investment strategy, investors need to assess their financial goals, risk tolerance, and the level of involvement they want in managing their investments. Seeking advice from financial professionals can also help in making well-informed decisions.

There are several ways to invest in the stock market, and the choice often depends on individual preferences, risk tolerance, and financial goals.

13. How To Invest In The Stock Market

When it comes to investing, individuals are frequently confronted with a pivotal decision: whether to manage their investments independently, leverage the services of Robo-Advisors, or entrust their portfolios to a professional financial advisor. Each option presents distinct advantages and disadvantages. In this chapter, we will delve into the pros and cons of each approach, offering valuable insights to assist you in making an informed decision.

i. Do-It-Yourself (DIY):

DIY investing is a strategy in which individual investors take control of their own investment decisions and manage their portfolios without relying on the services of a professional financial advisor.

The advantage of personally selecting your stock investments is that you can save on investment advisor fees. Additionally, you have complete control over your investment decisions, allowing you to choose specific stocks, bonds, or other securities based on your research and preferences.

Managing your investments independently provides an excellent opportunity to gain insights into financial markets, investment strategies, and risk management. This knowledge can be invaluable for personal finance in the long run.

While DIY investing offers individuals greater control over their investment decisions, it also comes with its set of challenges. Success in this approach necessitates a commitment to continuous education, dedicated time for research and analysis, and the ability to manage emotions amid market volatility.

Many investors opt out of the DIY route when considering the time involved. A friend once shared with me that he would rather allocate his precious time to higher priorities, such as family, health, or personal goals, than spend it on investment research and financial planning.

Ultimately, the decision to be a DIY investor hinges on individual financial knowledge, time commitment, risk tolerance, and investment goals. Some individuals find success in managing their own investments, while others prefer the guidance of financial professionals.

Do-It-Yourself (DIY) investing is also known as Self-Directed Investing.

ii. <u>Hire A Financial / Investment Advisor:</u>

A financial or investment advisor is a professional who is compensated for providing investment advice and managing the portfolios of their clients, either through a flat fee or a percentage of the assets they oversee.

One of the primary advantages of engaging a financial advisor is gaining access to their wealth of knowledge and experience. Advisors can navigate complex financial landscapes, identify investment opportunities, and offer valuable insights to help you make informed decisions. They can also assist in developing a comprehensive financial plan tailored to your specific goals, ensuring that, even in volatile times, your investment decisions are driven by logic rather than emotion.

However, these services come at a cost. Hiring a financial advisor typically involves a fee structure that may include management fees, commissions, or a percentage of assets under management. These costs can impact your returns, potentially diminishing the overall profitability of your investments. While most advisors are ethical and skilled, there is a risk of hiring a substandard advisor. It is recommended to ensure that, if you choose to hire a professional for managing your finances, they are fiduciary financial or investment advisors.

A fiduciary duty represents the highest standard of care. It mandates that the hired professional always acts in your best interest, with undivided loyalty and utmost good faith. A fiduciary financial advisor cannot recommend an investment that does not benefit you. Investors with fiduciary financial advisors can enjoy peace of mind, knowing that a trustworthy professional is monitoring their asset allocations, providing guidance on their overall investment strategy, and rebalancing their investment portfolio on their behalf.

iii.   Robo-Advisor:

Robo-advisors are automated investment platforms that utilize algorithms to create and manage diversified portfolios for investors. They operate by posing a few simple questions to ascertain your goals and risk tolerance, then invest your money in a highly diversified, low-cost portfolio of stocks and bonds. Robo-advisors continually rebalance your portfolio using algorithms.

For individuals with a basic understanding of investing who prefer not to spend time on research and management, a Robo-advisor allows them to put their investments on autopilot. Beyond selecting investments, it optimizes tax efficiency and automatically makes adjustments over time.

Robo-advisors typically charge significantly lower fees than financial advisors. However, it's essential to be aware of associated fees, such as management fees and investment expenses. Popular Robo-advisors include Nutmeg, Moneyfarm, Betterment, Wealthfront, Wealthsimple, Ellevest, and others.

Choosing among these three options depends on your goals, needs, knowledge, and current financial situation. To determine the right fit, consider the complexity of your finances, the amount of money you have to invest, the time you can allocate to investment research, and if necessary, seek professional advice.

A fiduciary duty represents the highest standard of care. It mandates that the hired professional always acts in your best interest, with undivided loyalty and utmost good faith.

14. Risk And Returns

Risk and returns are fundamental concepts in the world of stock market investing. They are closely related, and understanding their relationship is crucial for making informed investment decisions. When building an investment portfolio, there is an important balance to strike between risk and return. Typically, the higher the potential returns an investment can offer, the higher the risk it carries as well.

Higher long-term returns are compensation for investors taking on more volatility and uncertainty. For example, stocks have historically delivered higher average annual returns than bonds over long periods, but they also come with higher year-to-year volatility. The increased risk with stocks generates those larger gains. On the contrary, vehicles like high-yield savings accounts offer very low risk since your money is guaranteed. However, the trade-off is meagre returns.

As an investor, it is critical to understand your own risk tolerance level, investment timeline, and goals. These factors help determine how much risk is appropriate for you to assume in order to target your desired returns. Let's delve into a more detailed examination of the concepts of risks and returns.

Risks In Investing

Risk in investing refers to the potential for losing some or all of your invested capital. Understanding risks is essential for making informed investment decisions. Here are some common risks associated with investing in the stock market:

i.   Volatility Risk:

Volatility risk pertains to the fluctuations in the price of assets. Stock prices can be highly volatile, characterized by frequent and sometimes significant price swings. This volatility can create both opportunities and risks for investors, as rapid price changes may lead to gains or losses.

ii.   Market Risk:

Also known as 'systematic risk,' market risk refers to the overall volatility and unpredictability of the stock market. Factors such as economic conditions, recessions, geopolitical events, interest rates, and market sentiment can contribute to broad market fluctuations that affect the value of investments.

iii. Individual Stock Risk:

Every stock carries its own unique risks, encompassing company-specific factors like poor management decisions, declining sales, or legal issues. Investing in individual stocks can be riskier than diversifying across a range of companies or industries.

iv.   **Liquidity Risk:**

Liquidity risk refers to the difficulty of buying or selling a stock without significantly affecting its price. Some stocks may have lower trading volumes, making it challenging to execute large orders without impacting the stock's price.

v.   **Credit Risk:**

This risk applies primarily to bond investments. If you invest in companies with high levels of debt, you may be exposed to credit risk. Financial distress or defaults on debt obligations by the company can lead to a decline in the value of your investment.

vi.   **Interest Rate Risk:**

Changes in interest rates can impact the value of fixed-income investments, such as bonds. Rising interest rates can lead to lower stock prices as investors seek higher yields in other investment vehicles.

vii.   Inflation Risk:

Inflation erodes the purchasing power of money over time. If the returns on your investments do not outpace inflation, your real (inflation-adjusted) returns may be negative.

viii.   Political And Regulatory Risk:

Political events, changes in government policies, and regulatory decisions can affect markets and the value of investments, especially in regions with higher instability. This risk is particularly relevant for companies in highly regulated industries, such as healthcare or energy.

ix.   Currency Risk:

If you invest in assets denominated in foreign currencies, fluctuations in exchange rates can impact your returns. Exchange rate movements can lead to gains or losses when converting returns from one currency to another.

x.   Company Earnings And Dividend Risk:

Companies may experience fluctuations in earnings, leading to the possibility of reducing or eliminating dividend payments during challenging economic periods. Such changes can significantly impact the income generated from your investments.

xi. **Psychological And Behavioural Risks:**

Investor sentiment and behaviour have the potential to drive irrational market movements. Fear and greed can result in overvaluation (bubbles) or undervaluation (crashes) in the market.

It is crucial to recognize that all investments involve some level of risk, and there is no guaranteed method to completely eliminate these risks. Investors can effectively manage and mitigate these risks through diversification, thorough research, maintaining a long-term perspective, and adopting sound investment strategies aligned with their financial goals and risk tolerance.

When building an investment portfolio, there is an important balance to strike between risk and return.

Returns In Investing

Returns in investing denote the gains or losses produced from an investment within a specific timeframe. They can be positive (profits) or negative (losses) and are commonly expressed as a percentage of the initial investment, reflecting the investment's profitability or performance. Various types of stock market returns include:

i. **Capital Gains:**

Capital gains refer to the appreciation in the value of investments over time. Investors realize capital gains when the market value of their holdings increases, enabling them to sell shares at a profit.

For example, Nicky purchased 10 shares of Amazon stock on March 10, 2016, at £300 per share. Two years later, on March 10, 2018, she sold all the shares for £900 each. Assuming there were no fees associated with the sale, Nicky realized a capital gain of £6,000 ((£900 * 10) − (£300 * 10) = £6,000).

Capital gain is only possible when the selling price of the asset is greater than the original purchase price. It may be subject to taxation, with rates and exemptions varying between countries.

ii.   <u>Dividend Income:</u>

Some stocks pay dividends to shareholders as a portion of the company's profits. These regular payments can provide a steady stream of income in addition to potential capital appreciation. Dividend returns are often expressed as a percentage of the investment's current market price.

Most companies pay dividends in cash, although there may be instances where a company uses stock instead. It's important to understand that dividend payments are never guaranteed. Dividends are only distributed from a company's profits or reserves. Therefore, a loss-making company with no reserves cannot pay a dividend.

iii.   <u>Interest Income:</u>

Bonds and other fixed-income investments generate interest income, constituting a form of return.

Returns serve as a crucial metric for investors to assess their investment performance. Positive returns indicate profitability, while negative returns signify losses. Understanding and monitoring returns empower investors to evaluate the success of their investment strategy and make well-informed decisions regarding portfolio management.

15. Good Stock, Bad Stock: Investing Landscape

In the realm of finance and investing, the terms "good stock" and "bad stock" are frequently used, but what do they truly mean? The distinction between good and bad stocks is not always clear-cut, as it depends on various factors and the specific investment goals and risk tolerance of individual investors.

What Makes A Stock "Good"?

i. Strong Fundamentals:

Good stocks typically have strong fundamentals, including healthy revenue growth, solid earnings, and a robust balance sheet. Companies with a history of profitability and consistent growth tend to be considered good stocks.

ii. Competitive Advantage:

Companies that possess a sustainable competitive advantage, often referred to as an economic moat, are seen as having good stock potential. This advantage might come from proprietary technology, a dominant market position, or a well-known brand.

iii. Dividend Payments:

Some investors seek stocks that pay dividends. A company that consistently pays and increases its dividends over time is often viewed as a good investment, especially for income-focused investors.

iv. Management And Governance:

Strong and ethical corporate governance, along with competent management, are vital attributes of a good stock. Investors seek transparency and a management team that prioritizes shareholder interests.

v. Attractive Valuation:

A stock's price should be reasonable relative to its earnings and growth prospects. A stock considered good may be undervalued or reasonably priced based on metrics like the price-to-earnings (P/E) ratio.

vi. Diversification:

Building a diversified portfolio of stocks can reduce risk. Good stocks are often part of a well-balanced investment strategy that considers sector, industry, and asset class diversification.

vii. **Market Trends and Sentiment**:

Analyzing market trends and investor sentiment can help identify good stocks. Stocks in industries poised for growth, or those with positive news and sentiment, are often seen as good choices.

What Makes a Stock "Bad"?

i. **Weak Fundamentals:**

Stocks with poor financial performance, low or negative earnings, and mounting debt are often considered bad investments. Companies that consistently underperform or operate at a loss fall into this category.

ii. **Uncertain Future Prospects:**

Companies that lack a clear vision or strategy for future growth can be perceived as bad investments. This uncertainty may arise from market changes, technological disruptions, or ineffective management.

iii. **Scandals And Ethical Issues:**

Stocks of companies embroiled in scandals, ethical violations, or poor governance practices are usually seen as bad investments. Such issues erode trust and can have a lasting negative impact on stock value.

iv. <u>Overvaluation:</u>

Stocks that are significantly overpriced relative to their fundamentals are often considered bad investments. An excessively high P/E ratio or other valuation metrics can be a warning sign.

v. <u>No Dividend Or Inconsistent Payments:</u>

While not all investors prioritize dividends, a lack of consistent dividend payments can make a stock less attractive for income-focused investors.

vi. <u>High Volatility:</u>

Stocks that exhibit extreme price fluctuations, often associated with speculative investments, are generally seen as riskier and, by extension, bad stocks for conservative investors.

vii. <u>Limited Market Liquidity:</u>

Stocks that lack liquidity, making them difficult to buy or sell without significantly affecting the market price, are often deemed bad investments. This illiquidity can result in poor execution of trades and higher transaction costs.

The distinction between good and bad stocks is not black and white but rather a gradient that depends on various factors and an investor's individual objectives.

Identifying good stocks involves careful research, analysis, and an understanding of the company, its industry, and broader market conditions. Conversely, avoiding bad stocks requires vigilance in recognizing warning signs and red flags that indicate potential problems.

The stock market is dynamic, meaning today's good stock could be tomorrow's bad stock and vice versa. Regularly reviewing and updating your portfolio is vital to ensure you are aligned with your investment goals.

Remember, the key to successful investing lies not in chasing winners or avoiding losers, but in having a well-researched and diversified strategy that you stick to over the long term.

A well-balanced investment portfolio should consist of stocks that align with an investor's financial goals, risk tolerance, and time horizon.

PART 4:

DEEP DIVE INTO FINANCIAL INSTRUMENTS

---

16. Understanding Shares

Shares, also known as stocks or equity, represent ownership in a corporation or company. When you own shares of a company's stock, you become a shareholder and have a claim on a portion of that company's assets and earnings.

There are several types of shares available in the stock market, each with its unique characteristics and potential benefits and risks. Here are the common types of shares:

i. **Ordinary Shares:**

Also known as 'Common Shares' or 'Common Stock,' these represent basic ownership in a company. Holders of common shares have voting rights at shareholder meetings and may receive dividends, which are a portion of the company's profits distributed to shareholders.

Common shares are the most prevalent type of equity security and are traded on stock exchanges. However, they come with greater risk and uncertainty compared to other types of securities. Investors in common shares should be prepared for the possibility of market fluctuations and the absence of guaranteed dividends.

ii. <u>Preferred Shares:</u>

Also known as 'Preference Shares' or 'Preferred Stock', represent a class of ownership in a corporation and have characteristics of both common stocks and bonds. They often come with specific privileges; for example, preferred shareholders receive dividends before common shareholders and are paid a fixed dividend rate. However, they have limited or no voting rights compared to common shareholders.

Investors may be attracted to preferred shares for their relatively stable income stream and the priority they receive in terms of dividends and liquidation. However, they also come with some risks, such as the potential for the company to suspend dividend payments, and they may not offer the same potential for capital appreciation as common stocks.

iii. <u>Convertible Shares:</u>

Also known as 'Convertible Preferred Stock' or 'Convertible Securities,' these are a type of financial instrument that combines features of both debt and equity. Convertible shares give the holder the option to convert them into a predetermined number of common shares of the issuing company.

This financial instrument appeals to investors seeking a balance between income generation and the potential for capital appreciation. They are often issued by companies looking to raise capital without immediately diluting existing shareholders' equity. Investors should carefully consider the terms and conditions associated with convertible shares before making investment decisions.

iv. <u>**Restricted Shares:**</u>

Also known as 'Restricted Stock' or 'Restricted Stock Units (RSUs),' these are a form of equity compensation granted to employees by a company. These shares are subject to certain restrictions or conditions that must be met before the recipient gains full ownership and control over them.

Restricted shares are often a common component of employee compensation packages, especially for executives and key employees. They provide a way for companies to retain and reward talent while ensuring that employees have a vested interest in the company's performance over the long term. The specific terms and conditions of restricted share grants can vary widely from one company to another.

v.   **<u>Non-voting Shares:</u>**

Also known as 'Non-voting Stock' or 'Non-voting Equity', these are a class of shares in a company that typically do not carry the right to vote on certain matters affecting the company. While common shareholders usually have the right to vote on various corporate decisions, non-voting shareholders either have limited or no voting rights. Investors holding these shares may still benefit from dividends and capital appreciation but cannot participate in certain corporate decisions.

vi. **<u>Redeemable Shares:</u>**

Also known as 'Repurchasable Shares,' these are a type of share that a company can buy back from shareholders at a predetermined price. The ability to redeem shares is typically outlined in the company's articles of association or other governing documents.

It is important to note that the ability to issue redeemable shares and the terms associated with their redemption are subject to legal and regulatory requirements. Additionally, the specifics of redeemable shares can vary, and investors should carefully review the terms and conditions outlined in the company's governing documents before investing in such shares.

vii. **Participating Shares:**

These are a type of equity security that gives shareholders the right to receive additional dividends or other distributions beyond a predetermined amount. These shares allow shareholders to "participate" in the company's financial success by receiving extra benefits if certain conditions are met.

Participating shares are not as prevalent as common shares or preferred shares, and their features can vary from one company to another. These shares are often used in unique or specific situations, and their terms are typically detailed in the company's articles of association or other relevant legal documents. Investors considering participating shares should carefully review the terms and conditions associated with these shares to understand the potential benefits and risks.

viii. **Founder's Shares:**

These are the initial shares of a company that are typically issued to its founders or original owners at the time of its establishment. These shares are often given to individuals who played a significant role in the founding and early development of the company.

Founder's shares are a critical component of a start-up's early capital structure and can have significant implications for the governance and future financing of the company. As the company grows and attracts additional investors, the founder's shares may be subject to adjustments, and their terms could be revisited during subsequent funding rounds or events.

How Shares Work

Shares are bought and sold in financial markets, primarily through stock exchanges which are platforms where investors can trade shares. The price of shares fluctuates based on supply and demand dynamics, as well as various factors affecting the company's performance and the overall economy. Key concepts related to shares include:

i. **Initial Public Offering (IPO):**

When a private company decides to go public, it conducts an IPO, issuing shares to the public for the first time. This process allows the company to raise capital by selling ownership stakes.

ii. **Stock Price:**

Also known as the share price or equity price, it is the current market value of a single share of a company's stock. It represents the price at which investors can buy or sell shares in the open market. It is determined by the forces of supply and demand in the market.

iii. <u>Dividends:</u>

These are payments made by a company to its shareholders as a distribution of profits. Dividends are one of the ways in which companies share their earnings with investors. The payments are typically made in cash, although they can also be issued as additional shares of stock (stock dividends). Investors often consider dividends as a source of income and a key factor when evaluating the attractiveness of a stock.

iv. <u>Capital Gains:</u>

Shareholders can profit from shares by selling them at a higher price than their purchase price. This difference is known as capital gains. The gains can be categorized into two types: short-term capital gains and long-term capital gains, depending on how long the shares are held before they are sold.

v. <u>Risk:</u>

Investing in shares carries risks. Share prices can be volatile, and investors may lose money if the value of their shares decreases. It is important to conduct thorough research and diversify a portfolio to manage risk.

Significance Of Shares

Shares play a pivotal role in driving economic growth, providing a source of capital for companies, and offering individuals a pathway to wealth creation and financial security. Their significance extends to both the macroeconomic landscape and the financial well-being of individual investors. The list below shows the unique significance of shares:

i. **Capital Formation:**

Shares enable companies to raise capital by selling ownership stakes to investors. This capital can be used for various purposes, such as expanding operations, research and development, and debt repayment. Capital formation is essential for economic growth as it allows businesses to invest in new projects, create jobs, and contribute to overall economic development.

ii. **Investment Opportunities and Wealth Creation:**

Shares offer individuals and institutions the opportunity to invest in companies they believe in and potentially benefit from their growth and profitability. As companies grow and their share prices appreciate, the wealth of shareholders increases. This wealth effect can positively impact consumer confidence and spending, contributing to economic expansion.

iii. **Diversification:**

Shares provide a way for investors to diversify their investment portfolios, spreading risk across different companies, industries, and geographic regions. Diversification can help mitigate the impact of poor performance in any single investment.

iv. **Liquidity:**

Shares are highly liquid assets, meaning they can be bought or sold on stock exchanges relatively easily. This liquidity makes it possible for investors to convert their investments into cash when needed.

v. **Economic Health Indicators:**

The performance of stock markets and share prices are often used as economic indicators, reflecting the health of the overall economy. Rising share prices may indicate confidence in economic prospects, while falling prices may signal concerns or a potential economic downturn.

Investing in shares is a common way for individuals and institutions to participate in the financial markets and potentially benefit from the growth and profitability of publicly traded companies. It is important to conduct thorough research, consider your investment goals and risk tolerance, and diversify your portfolio when investing in shares. If needed, seek advice from financial professionals to make well-informed decisions tailored to your individual circumstances.

Shares play a pivotal role in driving economic growth, providing a source of capital for companies, and offering individuals a pathway to wealth creation and financial security.

17. Understanding Bonds

A bond is a debt instrument where the issuer (typically a government or corporation) borrows money from investors (bondholders) for a specified period, promising to repay the principal amount (the face value or par value) at maturity and make periodic interest payments along the way.

Bonds are considered a safer investment compared to stocks because they provide a predictable income stream and are generally less volatile. There are several types of bonds, each with its own characteristics. Here are some common types:

i. **<u>Government Bonds:</u>**

These are issued by governments to raise funds for various purposes, such as financing public projects, infrastructure development, or managing budget deficits. When you buy a government bond, you are essentially lending money to the government in exchange for periodic interest payments and the return of the principal amount at the bond's maturity.

Government bonds are considered one of the safest investments because they are backed by the taxing power of the government. However, they are not entirely risk-free. Factors such as inflation, interest rate changes, and economic conditions can affect the value of government bonds. Investors often include government bonds in their portfolios as a way to preserve capital and provide a stable source of income.

ii. **Corporate Bonds:**

These are debt securities issued by companies as a way to raise capital for various purposes, such as business expansion, debt refinancing, or other corporate needs. When investors purchase corporate bonds, they are essentially lending money to the issuing company in exchange for regular interest payments and the return of the principal amount at the bond's maturity.

Corporate bonds vary in risk depending on the issuer's creditworthiness, with higher-quality bonds being less risky and lower-yield bonds being riskier. The creditworthiness of the issuing company, economic conditions, and interest rate movements all play roles in determining the performance of corporate bonds.

iii. **Municipal Bonds:**

These are issued by state and local governments or their agencies. They are used to fund public projects like schools, highways, and infrastructure development. When investors purchase municipal bonds, they are essentially lending money to the issuing government entity in exchange for periodic interest payments and the return of the principal amount at maturity.

One of the main attractions of municipal bonds for investors is the potential for tax advantages. Interest income generated by most municipal bonds is typically exempt from federal income tax. Additionally, if an investor buys bonds issued by their state or locality, the interest income may also be exempt from state and local income taxes.

iv.   Treasury Bonds:

Often referred to as "T-bonds", they are long-term debt securities issued by the U.S. Department of the Treasury to raise funds for various government expenditures. These bonds are considered one of the safest investments because they are backed by the full faith and credit of the U.S. government.

Investors, including individuals, institutional investors, and foreign governments, are attracted to Treasury bonds because of their safety and stability. The interest payments and return on principal provide a predictable income stream for investors.

v.   Premium Bonds:

Premium Bonds are an investment product issued by National Savings and Investment (NS&I). Unlike other investments, where you earn interest or a regular dividend income, you are entered into a monthly prize draw where you can win between £25 and £1 million tax-free.

Premium Bonds offer a unique way for individuals to save money with the added excitement of potentially winning prizes. It's essential to note that, while some people may win significant prizes, others may not win anything at all in a given month. The returns are not guaranteed, making it a form of savings with an element of luck involved.

vi.   **Supranational Bonds:**

These are issued by international organizations like the World Bank, the European Investment Bank (EIB), the Asian Development Bank (ADB), etc. These entities transcend national borders and are typically created to address specific regional or global issues.

Supranational bonds are generally considered to have a strong credit quality because they are backed by the collective creditworthiness of the member countries. As a result, these bonds often receive high credit ratings, making them attractive to investors seeking a balance between risk and return.

vii.   <u>Convertible Bonds:</u>

Convertible bonds give bondholders the option to convert their bonds into a specified number of the issuer's common stock shares. These financial instruments have characteristics of both debt and equity, providing investors with potential capital appreciation along with regular interest payments.

viii.   <u>Mortgage-Backed Securities (MBS):</u>

MBS bonds represent an ownership interest in a pool of mortgages. They are created when financial institutions bundle individual mortgages together and sell them to investors. Investors receive payments based on the interest and principal payments from the underlying mortgage loans.

ix.   <u>Zero-Coupon Bonds:</u>

Also known as 'Discount Bonds' or 'Deep Discount Bonds', these are debt securities that do not make periodic interest payments like traditional bonds. Instead, they are issued at a discount to their face value and mature at par, meaning that the investor receives the face value of the bond when it reaches maturity. The difference between the purchase price and the face value represents the investor's return, and this return is a form of interest income.

These are just a few examples of bonds. The bond market is diverse, offering a wide range of instruments to meet the needs of investors and issuers with varying risk tolerance and investment objectives.

Bonds are considered a safer investment compared to stocks because they provide a predictable income stream and are generally less volatile.

How Bonds Work

Bonds work as a form of debt financing where the bondholder lends money to the issuer in exchange for periodic interest payments and the return of the principal amount at maturity. Here is a step-by-step explanation of how bonds work:

i.   Issuance:

A government, corporation, municipality, or other entity in need of capital decides to raise funds by issuing bonds. The issuer specifies the terms of the bonds, including the face value, coupon rate, maturity date, and other relevant features.

ii.   Sale To Investors:

The bonds are then offered to investors in the primary market through an initial bond offering. Investors purchase the bonds at the issuance price, which can be at par (equal to face value), at a premium (above face value), or a discount (below face value).

iii.   Coupon Rate:

The coupon rate is the annual or semi-annual interest rate that the issuer pays to bondholders, expressed as a percentage of the face value. For example, a bond with a face value of £1,000 and a 5% coupon rate pays £50 in annual interest.

iv.   Maturity Date:

Bonds have a fixed maturity date, at which point the issuer repays the principal amount (face value) to the bondholders. The maturity period can range from a few months to several decades, depending on the type of bond.

v.   Face Value Redemption:

The face value of a bond is the amount the issuer will repay to the bondholder at maturity. It is also the amount used to calculate interest payments. This return of principal is one of the key features of bonds.

vi.   Yield:

The yield represents the return an investor can expect to receive from a bond, taking into account the bond's current market price, coupon rate, and time to maturity. It is typically expressed as a percentage of the current yield or yield to maturity (YTM).

vii.   Market Price:

The market price of a bond fluctuates based on interest rates, the creditworthiness of the issuer, and other market conditions. If the market price of a bond rises above its face value, it is said to be trading at a premium; if it falls below face value, it is trading at a discount.

Investors often include bonds in their portfolios for diversification and to balance the risk associated with other investment classes like stocks.

Significance Of Bonds

Bonds play a crucial role in financial markets, providing a source of financing for governments and corporations and offering investors a way to generate income and manage risk. Here are some of the key significance and roles of bonds:

i.   **Capital Formation:**

Bonds provide a source of capital for governments and corporations to finance projects and operations. By issuing bonds, these entities can tap into a diverse pool of investors to secure the funds necessary for their initiatives. They are a crucial tool for raising large amounts of money.

ii.   **Income Generation:**

Bonds offer a steady stream of interest income to investors, making them an attractive option for those seeking stable returns, especially those in or near retirement who may rely on fixed-income investments for living expenses.

iii.   **Diversification:**

Bonds play a crucial role in diversifying an investment portfolio and balancing the risk associated with stocks and other assets. Their characteristics, such as fixed income, lower volatility compared to stocks, and potential capital preservation, make them an essential component for investors aiming to manage risk and achieve a balanced portfolio.

iv.   Interest Rate Benchmark:

The yields on government bonds, particularly those with longer maturities, often serve as benchmarks for interest rates in the broader economy. Changes in bond yields can influence borrowing costs for businesses and individuals, affecting economic activity.

v.   Retirement Planning:

Bonds can be a key component of retirement planning for individuals. Their fixed-income nature and lower risk profile relative to stocks make them attractive for conservative investors or those looking to preserve capital as they approach retirement.

vi.   Simplicity:

Bonds are relatively simple to understand compared to more complex securities. This facilitates easier trading and management.

Overall, bonds serve a valuable function in investment portfolios by providing steady income, diversification benefits, and relative stability. Their significance comes from complementing riskier assets like stocks. The dynamics of the bond market can have far-reaching effects on the broader economy, making bonds an integral component of the global financial system.

18. Understanding Other Derivatives: Options

Options are financial instruments that give the holder the right (but not the obligation) to buy or sell an underlying asset at a predetermined price (strike price) within a specified period (expiration date). Options are a type of derivative, meaning their value is derived from the value of an underlying asset, such as stocks, indices, commodities, or currencies. There are two main types of stock options: call options and put options.

A call option gives the buyer the right to purchase a specified number of shares at the strike price before or at the expiration date. The seller (writer) of the call option is obligated to sell the stock if the buyer chooses to exercise the option.

A put option gives the buyer the right to sell a specified number of shares at the strike price before or at the expiration date. The seller (writer) of the put option is obligated to buy the stock if the buyer chooses to exercise the option.

Uses Of Options

Options are versatile financial instruments that offer various uses for investors and traders. Here are some common uses of options:

i. Speculation:

Investors can use options to speculate on the price movements of underlying assets without owning the assets themselves. Buying call options in anticipation of a price increase or buying put options in anticipation of a price decrease are speculative strategies.

ii. Hedging:

Options can be used as a risk management tool to hedge against potential losses in a portfolio. Investors holding a portfolio of stocks can purchase put options to protect against potential losses in the value of their stocks. If the stock prices fall, the gains from the put options can offset the losses in the stock portfolio.

iii. Income Generation:

Option sellers can generate income by collecting premiums from buyers, especially in stable or low-volatility markets. Selling call options against a stock position allows investors to generate income through the premiums received. If the stock price remains below the strike price, the investor keeps the premium as profit.

iv.   **Strategies:**

Various option trading strategies, such as covered calls, protective puts, straddles, and spreads, can be employed based on market expectations. Strategies like buying both a call and a put (straddle) or purchasing out-of-the-money call and put options (strangle) aim to profit from significant price movements, regardless of the direction.

It is important to note that while options can offer strategic benefits, they also involve risks, and investors should thoroughly understand the mechanics of options trading before incorporating them into their investment strategies. Additionally, options trading is not suitable for all investors, and individuals should carefully consider their risk tolerance and investment objectives.

19. Understanding Other Derivatives: Futures

Futures are financial derivatives that obligate the buyer to purchase or the seller to sell an underlying asset at a predetermined price on a specified future date. These contracts are standardized and traded on organized exchanges, with specific terms, including the quantity and quality of the underlying asset, expiration date, and the agreed-upon price (known as the futures price or strike price).

Key Features Of Futures

Here are some of the key features of Futures:

i. **Standardization:**

Futures contracts are highly standardized, with terms set by the exchange. This includes the size of the contract, expiration date, and how price changes are settled.

ii. **Expiration Date:**

Futures contracts have a specified expiration date, after which the contract is no longer valid. Most futures contracts expire on a monthly or quarterly basis.

iii.   Underlying Assets:

The underlying assets of a futures contract can be diverse, including commodities (e.g., oil, gold), financial instruments (e.g., stock indices, interest rates), or even specific commodities like agricultural products.

iv.   Margin Requirements:

Both the buyer (long position) and the seller (short position) are required to deposit a margin with the exchange. This margin serves as collateral and helps ensure that both parties fulfil their obligations.

v.   Daily Settlement:

Futures contracts are marked to market daily, meaning gains and losses are settled each day. This process helps manage the risk of default and ensures that both parties have adequate margins.

vi.   Delivery Vs. Cash Settlement:

While some futures contracts result in the physical delivery of the underlying asset, many are cash-settled. In a cash settlement, the difference in value is paid in cash rather than delivering the actual asset.

vii.   **Regulation:**

Futures markets are subject to regulatory oversight to ensure fair and transparent trading practices. Regulatory bodies oversee futures markets to prevent fraud and manipulation.

Uses Of Futures

Futures contracts serve various purposes for market participants, including hedging, speculation, portfolio management, and risk mitigation. Here are some common uses of futures:

i.   **Speculation:**

Traders can use futures contracts to speculate on the price movements of underlying assets without owning the assets themselves. This can provide opportunities for profit, but it also involves risk.

ii.   **Hedging:**

Businesses and investors use futures contracts to hedge against price fluctuations in the underlying asset. For example, a farmer might use futures contracts to lock in the price of crops before harvest.

iii. <u>Leverage:</u>

Futures contracts allow traders to control a large amount of an underlying asset with a relatively small upfront investment, providing leverage. While this can amplify returns, it also increases the potential for losses.

iv. <u>Price Discovery:</u>

The prices of futures contracts are often used as indicators of market sentiment and expectations about future prices of the underlying assets. They contribute to the price discovery process.

v. <u>Portfolio Diversification:</u>

Investors and fund managers use futures contracts to adjust their portfolio exposure, manage risk, and achieve specific investment objectives.

While futures offer various benefits, it's crucial to note that they also involve risks, including the potential for significant financial losses. It requires a good understanding of the markets, risk management strategies, and the ability to monitor positions actively. Investors should carefully consider their risk tolerance and investment objectives before participating in futures markets.

PART 5:

MANAGING INVESTMENT PORTFOLIO

20. What Is A Brokerage Firm?

Brokerage firms, also known as 'Brokerage Houses' or 'Brokerage Companies', are financial institutions that facilitate the buying and selling of financial securities on behalf of clients. I like to refer to them as an intermediary or a middleman who connects buyers and sellers to complete a transaction for stock shares, bonds, mutual funds, exchange-traded funds (ETFs), options, and other investment products.

Well-known brokerage firms include Vanguard, Hargreaves Lansdown, AJ Bell Youinvest, Charles Schwab, Fidelity Investments, TD Ameritrade, E*TRADE, Interactive Brokers, Robinhood, and many more. Investors often choose a brokerage based on factors such as the range of investment options, fees, customer service, and the overall user experience. Here are key points about brokerage firms:

i.   **Intermediaries:**

Brokerage firms serve as intermediaries between buyers and sellers in financial markets. When an investor wants to buy or sell a security, they place an order with a brokerage firm, which then executes the trade on a stock exchange or other trading venue.

ii.   Services:

Brokerage firms provide various services to investors, ranging from executing trades to offering investment advice and research. The level of services can vary widely, with some brokerages providing full-service offerings that include personalized financial advice, while others focus on online trading with fewer advisory services.

iii.   Online And Traditional Brokerages:

With the advent of the internet, online brokerages have become increasingly popular. These platforms allow investors to place trades, access research and market information, and manage their portfolios online. Traditional or full-service brokerages may have physical branch locations and offer a broader range of services, including financial planning and wealth management.

iv.   Commission And Fee Structure:

Brokerage firms typically charge fees and commissions for their services. However, there has been a trend toward commission-free trading in recent years, especially among online brokerages. We discussed some of these fees in Chapter 24. It is essential for investors to comprehend the fee structure and any associated costs when selecting a brokerage.

v. **Regulation:**

Brokerage firms are subject to financial regulations and oversight by regulatory authorities in the countries where they operate. Regulatory oversight ensures that brokerages adhere to industry standards, operate fairly, and protect the interests of investors.

vi. **Investment Products:**

Brokerage firms offer a wide range of investment products, allowing investors to diversify their portfolios. These products include stocks, bonds, mutual funds, ETFs, options, and more.

vii. **Account Management:**

Brokerages manage client accounts, including holding securities, processing dividends and interest payments, and providing regular statements of account activity.

viii. **Risk and Reward:**

Investing through a brokerage involves risks, and the value of investments can fluctuate. While brokerage firms provide tools and information to help investors make informed decisions, it is essential for investors to thoroughly understand the risks associated with their investment choices.

Before selecting a brokerage, investors should carefully consider their investment goals, the level of service they require, and the associated fees and commissions. It is essential to research and compare different brokerages to find the one that best aligns with individual preferences and financial objectives.

Well-known brokerage firms include Vanguard, Hargreaves Lansdown, AJ Bell Youinvest, Charles Schwab, Fidelity Investments, TD Ameritrade, E*TRADE, Interactive Brokers, Robinhood, and many more.

21. Opening A Brokerage Account

A brokerage account is a financial platform that enables individuals to buy and sell various financial assets, including stocks, bonds, mutual funds, exchange-traded funds (ETFs), options, and more. To participate in the stock market, obtaining a brokerage account is essential. These accounts are offered by brokerage firms and function as conduits for investors to access financial markets and execute trades.

Brokerage accounts come in various types, including individual accounts, joint accounts, retirement or personal pension accounts, and custodial accounts for minors. Each type of account has its own set of rules and tax implications. Opening a brokerage account is easily done online; typically, it's a quick and straightforward process that takes only a few minutes.

Similar to a regular bank account, you can easily transfer money into and out of a brokerage account. Additionally, you will have access to the stock market and other investment opportunities. You don't need a significant amount of money to open a brokerage account. In fact, many brokerage firms allow you to open an account with no initial deposit. However, you will need to fund the account before making investments, and you can do so by transferring money from your current or savings account, or from another investment account.

Here are general steps to guide you through the process of opening a brokerage account:

i. **Determine Your Investment Goals And Needs:**

    Before opening a brokerage account, assess your financial goals, risk tolerance, and investment strategy. Are you investing for wealth building, retirement, short-term gains, or something else? Understanding your needs will help you choose the right brokerage and account type.

ii. **Research Brokerage Firms:**

    Explore different brokerage firms to find one that aligns with your investment needs. Consider factors such as fees, available investment options, research tools, and customer service. Read reviews and compare offerings to make an informed choice. Popular online brokerages include Vanguard, Charles Schwab, Fidelity, TD Ameritrade, E*TRADE, and others.

iii. **Visit The Brokerage Website:**

    Once you have chosen a brokerage, visit its official website. Look for an "Open an Account" or similar button/link on the homepage. Most brokerages offer online account opening processes, allowing you to apply via their website or mobile app. Some may also offer in-person account openings at physical branches.

iv.   Choose The Account Type:

Most brokerages offer various types of accounts, including individual accounts, joint accounts, general accounts, junior/custodial accounts, Stocks and Shares ISAs accounts, retirement/pension accounts (SIPPs, IRAs), and more. Select the account type that aligns with your financial goals and tax considerations.

v.   Fill Out The Application Form:

Complete the online application form. You'll need to provide personal information such as your name, address, national insurance number or social security number, employment information, and financial details. Be prepared to answer questions about your investment experience, financial goals, and risk tolerance. Provide accurate information and details as requested.

vi.   Agree To Terms And Conditions:

Review the terms and agreements carefully. This may include information about fees, commissions, privacy policy, and other account-related details. Ensure that you understand and agree to the terms.

vii.   <u>**Verify Your Identity:**</u>

As part of the account opening process, you may need to confirm your identity by providing additional documentation, such as a driver's license or passport.

viii.   <u>**Fund Your Account:**</u>

Once your account is approved, you will need to deposit funds to start investing. Brokerages offer various funding methods, such as bank transfers, wire transfers, and check deposits. Some also accept electronic fund transfers from linked bank accounts.

ix.   <u>**Select Investments:**</u>

Once your account is funded, you can start investing. Explore the available investment options, including stocks, bonds, mutual funds, ETFs, and more. Execute buy or sell orders through the brokerage's trading platform.

x.   <u>**Set Up Account Preferences:**</u>

Customize your account preferences, including notifications, statement delivery methods, and other settings to suit your needs.

xi.   <u>**Monitor And Manage Your Investments:**</u>

Keep a vigilant eye on your investments, periodically review your portfolio, and adjust your strategy as needed to align with your financial goals. Many brokerages provide tools to help you track your investments and monitor market trends.

xii.   <u>**Stay Informed:**</u>

Keep up-to-date with market news, economic developments, and changes in your investment portfolio. Many brokerages offer research tools and educational resources to help you make informed decisions.

Different brokerage firms have different account minimums, fees, and features. It is essential to compare your options and choose a brokerage that aligns with your investment style and objectives. There is no legal limit to the number of brokerage accounts you can have or the amount of money you can deposit into a brokerage account each year. In some cases, having multiple brokerage accounts could be the best move for your financial situation.

Investors have the option to open taxable brokerage accounts or tax-advantaged accounts like Stocks & Shares ISAs (UK) and Roth IRAs (US). This provides flexibility in managing taxes. In the UK, Stock and Shares Individual

Savings Accounts (ISA) allow investors to invest in a wide range of shares, funds, investment trusts and bonds without paying income tax or capital gains tax on the money earned from the investments, up to a certain limit (currently £20,000 at the time of writing this book – October 2023).

Roth IRA (Individual Retirement Account) is the USA's closest equivalent of the UK Stock and Shares ISA in terms of tax-advantaged accounts designed to encourage saving and investing. Contributions to a Roth IRA are made with after-tax dollars, meaning you don't get a tax deduction for your contributions. The earnings on investments within the Roth IRA also grow tax-free, and qualified withdrawals from a Roth IRA are tax-free. The Roth IRA has an annual contribution limit. This limit can change based on various factors, such as income and age.

You don't need a lot of money to open a brokerage account. In fact, many brokerage firms allow you to open an account with no initial deposit.

22. Creating An Investing Portfolio

An investment portfolio is a collection of assets, such as stocks, bonds, exchange-traded funds (ETFs), real estate, and other investment instruments, carefully selected and managed to achieve specific financial objectives. The composition of an investment portfolio is typically based on the investor's financial goals, risk tolerance, and investment time horizon - tailored to individual preferences and financial circumstances.

Some investors may prefer a more conservative portfolio with a higher allocation to fixed-income securities (bonds), while others with a longer time horizon and higher risk tolerance may favour a more aggressive portfolio with a larger allocation to equities (stocks). Whether you are planning for retirement, saving for a major purchase, or just looking to grow your wealth, creating an investment portfolio is a crucial step in securing your financial future.

Here are some general steps to help you create an investment portfolio:

i. Define Your Investment Goals:

Before you begin building your investment portfolio, it is essential to define your investment goals. Your goals will influence your investment strategy. Common investment goals include:

- Retirement planning
- Buying a home
- Paying for education
- Generating regular income
- Growing wealth over the long term

Each of these goals may require a different investment approach and time horizon. Being clear about your goals is the first step in creating a successful portfolio.

ii.   **Risk Tolerance Assessment:**

Understanding your risk tolerance is crucial in portfolio construction. Risk tolerance is a measure of how comfortable you are with fluctuations in the value of your investments. It is essential to strike a balance between risk and return.

High-risk investments often have the potential for high returns but come with higher volatility. Low-risk investments tend to be more stable but offer lower returns. The general rule of thumb is to invest in riskier assets (e.g., stocks) when you are young and have time to recover from downturns. As you get older, consider moving some of your invested money to safer investments (e.g., bonds) with a lower potential rate of return but less chance of losing it all.

iii. Diversification:

Diversification is a fundamental principle of creating a resilient investment portfolio. It involves spreading investments across different asset classes, industries, sectors, and geographic regions. This strategy helps manage risk by reducing the impact of poor performance in any one investment.

Asset classes can include stocks, bonds, real estate, and alternative investments like commodities or private equity. Diversification helps you avoid putting all your eggs in one basket. A diversified portfolio can better withstand market fluctuations and economic downturns.

iv. Asset Allocation:

Asset allocation is the process of deciding how much of your portfolio should be allocated to different asset classes like stocks, bonds, etc. The right asset allocation depends on your investment goals, time horizon, and risk tolerance.

For example, a long-term investor with a higher risk tolerance might allocate a more significant portion of their portfolio to stocks, whereas a conservative investor might allocate more to bonds. Asset allocation is a crucial strategic decision that aims to balance risk and return based on an investor's objectives.

v. Investment Selection:

Once you've determined your asset allocation, it's time to choose specific investments in your portfolio. Consider factors like:

- Individual stocks and bonds.
- Mutual funds and Exchange Traded Funds (ETFs).
- Real Estate Investment Trusts (REITs).
- Commodities or precious metals.

These investment vehicles offer different levels of diversification and management styles. It is essential to conduct thorough research, considering historical performance, fees, and the quality of the assets you are investing in.

vi. Long-term Perspective:

A successful investment portfolio is often designed with a long-term perspective. Long-term investing allows for the potential benefits of compounding and helps smooth out the impact of short-term market volatility.

vii. Regular Monitoring and Rebalancing

Creating an investment portfolio is not a one-time task. It requires ongoing monitoring and periodic rebalancing. Market conditions change, and your financial goals might evolve. Rebalancing involves adjusting the portfolio periodically to maintain the desired asset allocation. It may involve buying or selling assets to bring the portfolio back in line with the investor's strategic plan. This ensures that your portfolio remains in line with your risk tolerance and goals.

viii.   <u>Seek Professional Advice</u>

Managing an investment portfolio can be complex, and the financial markets are influenced by a multitude of factors. Consider seeking advice from a financial advisor or investment professional, especially if you are unfamiliar with the intricacies of investing. They can help you make informed decisions and provide guidance on your specific financial situation.

Creating an investment portfolio is a dynamic and essential aspect of managing your finances. The portfolio created can be customized based on an individual's financial situation, goals, and risk tolerance. Whether managed independently or with the assistance of a financial advisor, the construction and management of a well-diversified portfolio are crucial elements of a successful investment strategy.

23. Tracking And Evaluating Your Investments

The key to successful investing doesn't end with making informed decisions and diversifying your portfolio. Regularly tracking and evaluating your investments is essential to ensure that your financial goals remain within reach and to adjust strategies as necessary. This is a crucial aspect of managing your portfolio effectively.

The Importance of Tracking and Evaluating

Tracking and evaluating investments are crucial components of effective financial management. The below points highlight the importance of these practices:

i.   **Performance Monitoring:**

Regular tracking allows you to monitor the performance of your investments over time. By assessing how well your portfolio is doing, you can make informed decisions about whether to maintain, adjust, or divest certain assets.

ii. **Goal Alignment:**

Regular evaluations ensure that your portfolio aligns with your financial objectives. Whether you are saving for retirement, a home purchase, education, or other objectives, tracking your investments helps you gauge progress toward those goals.

iii. **Risk Management:**

Tracking your investments enables you to assess the level of risk in your portfolio. Understanding the risk associated with each investment and the overall portfolio helps you make adjustments to maintain an acceptable level of risk based on your risk tolerance.

iv. **Asset Allocation Adjustment:**

Asset allocation is a key determinant of portfolio performance. Regular tracking enables you to maintain your desired asset allocation. If certain assets have deviated from your target allocation due to market movements, rebalancing can help bring your portfolio back in line with your strategic plan.

v. **Tax Planning:**

Monitoring your investments helps you stay aware of any tax implications. Understanding the tax consequences of selling or holding onto investments allows you to make tax-efficient decisions, potentially minimizing your tax liability.

vi.   Opportunity Identification:

Through regular evaluation, you may identify new investment opportunities or trends in the market. Staying informed allows you to capitalize on potential opportunities or adjust your portfolio to mitigate risks.

vii.   Behavioural Discipline:

Regularly monitoring your investments can help instil discipline in your investment approach. It discourages impulsive decisions driven by short-term market fluctuations and encourages a long-term perspective aligned with your financial goals.

viii.   Financial Awareness:

Tracking investments enhances financial awareness. Understanding the performance of your assets, market conditions, and economic trends contributes to a deeper comprehension of your overall financial situation.

ix.   Adaptability To Changing Circumstances:

Life circumstances change, and so do financial goals. Regular tracking enables you to adapt your investment strategy in response to changes in your personal or financial situation, ensuring that your portfolio remains in sync with your evolving needs.

x.   <u>Peace Of Mind:</u>

Knowing that you are actively managing and evaluating your investments can provide peace of mind. It offers a sense of control and confidence in your financial decisions.

Tracking and evaluating investments are essential for maintaining a healthy and effective investment portfolio. These practices empower you to make informed decisions, manage risks, and stay on course toward achieving your financial objectives. Regular assessments contribute to financial stability and increase the likelihood of long-term investment success.

The key to successful investing doesn't end with making informed decisions and diversifying your portfolio. Regularly tracking and evaluating your investments is essential to ensure that your financial goals remain within reach and to adjust strategies as necessary.

Investments Tracking Tools

There are several investment tracking tools and platforms available that can help you monitor and manage your investments more effectively. These tools often provide features such as portfolio tracking, performance analysis, and insights into market trends. Here are some popular investment tracking tools:

i. Personal Finance Apps:

Apps like Mint, Money Dashboard, and YNAB (You Need A Budget) are personal finance apps that allow you to link your investment accounts, prepare a budget, track your spending, and monitor your overall financial health. These tools provide a holistic view of your finances, including investments, savings, and debt.

ii. Brokerage Platforms:

Many brokerage platforms offer built-in tools for tracking and managing investments. For example, Fidelity, Vanguard, and many other brokerages provide a variety of tools for portfolio analysis, performance tracking, and access to educational resources. Many also provide regular statements, either monthly or quarterly. These documents offer insights into your holdings, recent transactions, and performance.

iii. **<u>Investment Tracking Software:</u>**

There are many dedicated software solutions and apps that aggregate your investment data, visualize performance, and even provide analytics. Trackers such as Morningstar Portfolio Manager are known for their investment research. The tool allows you to track your investments, analyze performance, and gain insights from Morningstar's research.

iv. **<u>Manual Spreadsheets:</u>**

For those who prefer a hands-on approach, creating a custom spreadsheet using software like Microsoft Excel or Google Sheets can be a flexible and tailored solution. You can use this tool to track your investments, calculate returns, and monitor your portfolio's performance.

v. **<u>News And Research Platforms:</u>**

Platforms like Yahoo Finance or Bloomberg not only provide news and financial information but also offer portfolio tracking tools. These platforms are useful for staying updated on market trends.

Remember to choose a tool that aligns with your needs, preferences, and the type of investments you hold. Additionally, ensure that the platform prioritizes security and privacy, especially when linking financial accounts.

Key Metrics For Evaluating Investment Performance

Evaluating investment performance involves considering various metrics that provide insights into how well your investments are doing. Here are key metrics commonly used to assess investment performance:

i.   Total Return:

This metric combines income (like dividends or interest) and capital appreciation to show the full performance of an investment.

ii.   Annualized Return:

An important metric that represents the average annual rate of return on an investment over a specified period. It is useful for comparing the performance of investments with different holding periods.

iii. Benchmark Comparison:

This metric compares your portfolio's performance against a relevant benchmark, like the S&P 500 or a bond index, to gauge how well you are doing relative to the market.

iv. Dividend Yield:

This metric measures the annual dividend income as a percentage of the investment's current market price. It is relevant for income-focused investments like dividend-paying stocks or bonds.

v. Beta:

Beta measures an investment's sensitivity to market movements. A beta of 1 indicates that the investment tends to move with the market, while a beta greater than 1 suggests higher volatility, and a beta less than 1 suggests lower volatility.

vi. Expense Ratio:

The expense ratio reflects the percentage of a fund's assets used to cover its operating expenses. Lower expense ratios are generally favourable for investors.

vii.   **Turnover Ratio:**

Turnover ratio measures the frequency with which assets in a portfolio are bought and sold. High turnover may lead to higher transaction costs.

viii.   **Price-to-Earnings (P/E) Ratio:**

For stocks, the P/E ratio compares the current market price to the company's earnings per share. It helps assess whether a stock is overvalued or undervalued.

It is essential to consider a combination of these metrics to obtain a comprehensive view of investment performance. No single metric provides a complete picture, so utilizing multiple indicators in conjunction with one another is often helpful. Additionally, the choice of metrics may depend on the type of investment (e.g., stocks, bonds, mutual funds) and the investor's specific goals and preferences.

Effective performance evaluation
is a middle ground between a
"set it and forget it"
and incessant monitoring.
A yearly evaluation of your
investments, preferably at the
same time each year, is often
sufficient. This approach allows
for a meaningful assessment
while avoiding unnecessary
reactionary decisions.

24. Investing Costs And Fees

Investing in financial markets comes with various costs and fees that investors should be aware of. These costs can significantly impact your overall returns, so understanding them is crucial when managing your investment portfolio. Fees act as an impediment to compounding; the more paid in fees, the less there is to compound into the future.

Below is a list of common fees associated with stock market investing:

i. **Brokerage Commissions:**

When buying or selling stocks, bonds, or other securities, investors often incur brokerage commissions. This fee may be a fixed amount per trade or a percentage of the transaction value. While many online brokerage platforms now offer commission-free trades, it is essential to be aware of any additional fees that may apply.

ii. **Management Fees:**

For those investing in mutual funds or exchange-traded funds (ETFs), an annual fee is typically paid to the fund manager for managing and operating the fund. This fee, known as the expense ratio, is expressed as a percentage of the fund's assets under management (AUM).

iii.   Advisory Fees:

If you engage a financial advisor or investment manager, they may charge advisory fees for their services. These fees can take the form of a fixed amount, a percentage of assets under management, or a combination of both.

iv.   Front-End And Back-End Loads:

Certain mutual funds impose sales loads, fees paid when buying (front-end load) or selling (back-end load) the fund. Typically expressed as a percentage of the amount invested, these loads can impact your initial investment or sale proceeds.

v.   Custodial Fees:

Using a custodian to hold and safeguard your investments may incur custodial fees. These fees can vary and are often charged on a regular basis.

vi.   Account Maintenance Fees:

Some brokerage accounts may have account maintenance fees, which are charged periodically (e.g., monthly, or annually) to cover the cost of maintaining your account.

vii. **Inactivity Fees:**

Some brokers impose inactivity fees if you fail to make a specified number of trades or maintain a minimum account balance within a set timeframe.

viii. **Transfer And Withdrawal Fees:**

Transferring investments to a different brokerage or withdrawing funds from your account may incur transfer or withdrawal fees. These fees can vary depending on the broker.

ix. **Taxes:**

Depending on your investment activity and the tax laws in your country, you may be subject to capital gains taxes when you sell investments at a profit. Tax implications can impact your overall returns.

x. **Exchange Fees:**

When trading on stock exchanges, you may be charged exchange fees. While these fees are typically low, they can accumulate for high-frequency traders.

xi. **Margin Interest:**

If you use margin (borrowed money) to invest, you will pay interest on the borrowed funds. The interest rate varies depending on your broker and the amount borrowed.

xii.   **<u>Currency Conversion Fees:</u>**

Investing in foreign securities or ETFs denominated in a different currency may lead to fees for currency conversion when buying or selling those assets.

It is crucial to review and understand the fee structure associated with your chosen investment products and services. These fees can vary significantly between brokers and investment vehicles, making it essential to compare costs for informed decision-making. Additionally, consider the impact of fees on your investment returns, as opting for lower-cost options can potentially enhance your long-term performance.

Fees act as an impediment to compounding; the more paid in fees, the less there is to compound into the future.

Impact Of Fees On Investment Returns

Being mindful of fees is paramount when investing in the stock market. These fees can significantly erode your investment returns over time, and for long-term investors, the impact can be substantial. Whilst you can't influence the performance of your investments, you can influence your returns by keeping your fees low. The difference between an annual fee of 0.6% and a 1% charge per year may seem negligible, but it adds up over time.

Let us consider an example. Assume you invest $20,000, and your yearly return is 7.5%. After 20 years, with the power of compound interest (interest earned on interest), you would have $84,957. However, if you are paying an annual fee of 1%, your returns would be around $14,484 less, resulting in $70,473.

On the other hand, with a lower annual fee of 0.6%, your returns would be $75,955 after two decades, keeping an extra $5,482 compared to when you had to pay a 1% fee. Keeping your investment costs to a minimum definitely leads to higher potential returns.

Here's the return you would see over 20 years:

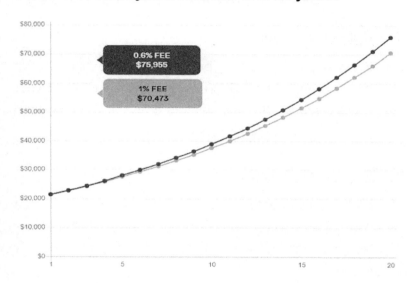

Here's what you would have to pay in fees over 20 years:

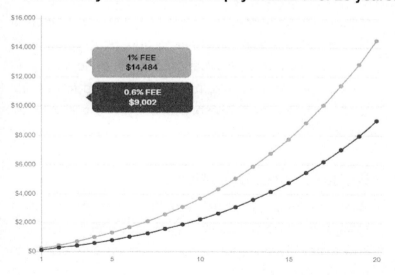

Some key insights on investing fees:

i. <u>Cost Over Time:</u>

Even seemingly small fees, when compounded over many years, can lead to a significant reduction in your overall returns. It is essential to consider the long-term impact of fees on your investment portfolio.

ii. <u>Erosion Of Returns:</u>

High fees can eat into your investment gains, making it more challenging to achieve your financial goals. Lower fees can help preserve a more significant portion of your profits.

iii. <u>Differing Fee Structures:</u>

Various investment products and services have different fee structures. It is essential to understand how fees work for the specific investments you choose, including brokerage commissions, management fees for mutual funds or ETFs, and advisory fees if you use a financial advisor.

iv. <u>Comparing Investment Options:</u>

When evaluating investment options, consider the fees along with other factors like historical performance, risk, and suitability for your goals. Lower-cost investments may provide a more attractive risk-adjusted return.

v. **Fee Transparency:**

Ensure you have a clear understanding of all fees associated with your investments, including any hidden or additional charges. Read the fine print and seek clarification from your broker or financial advisor if necessary.

vi. **Fee Negotiation:**

Depending on your relationship with your broker or advisor, you may be able to negotiate fees. It's worth exploring opportunities to reduce costs, especially if you have a substantial investment portfolio.

vii. **Regular Fee Monitoring:**

Fees can change over time, so it is essential to periodically monitor your investment costs. As your portfolio grows, even small changes in fees can result in significant differences in your returns.

In conclusion, while fees are a crucial aspect of investing, they should not be the sole determining factor when making stock market investment decisions. Investing is about finding the right balance between cost and the quality of the investment.

Lowering fees can enhance your returns, but it is equally important to focus on building a diversified and well-structured portfolio that aligns with your financial goals and risk tolerance. Always stay informed and make investment choices that are in your best financial interest.

While fees are a crucial aspect of investing, they should not be the sole determining factor when making stock market investment decisions. Investing is about finding the right balance between cost and the quality of the investment.

PART 6:

INVESTING STRATEGIES

25.   Active And Passive Investing

Active and passive investing are two broad approaches to managing investment portfolios. They differ in their strategies, goals, and the level of involvement of the investor or fund manager.

<u>Active Investing</u>

Active investing is an investment strategy where the investor or fund manager actively makes decisions to buy and sell securities with the goal of outperforming the overall market or a specific benchmark. This approach involves regular monitoring of market conditions, economic trends, and individual companies to identify opportunities for capitalizing on price movements.

Active investors often use quantitative and technical analysis, including ratio analysis, stock chart analysis and other mathematical measures to determine whether to buy or sell. The investment horizon can be months, days or even hours or minutes. Active investors look at the price movements of the investment many times a day with the motive of seeking short-term profits.

It's worth noting that active investing requires someone to act in the role of Portfolio or Active Money Manager. The goal of this investment expert is to beat the stock market's average returns and be able to immediately take advantage of short-term price fluctuations. While active money managers argue they will perform better in a rising market, they also contend that they will lose less in a falling market.

Benefits Of Active Investing

Active investing offers several potential benefits for investors. Here are some of the advantages associated with active investment strategies:

i. Short-Term Opportunities:

Investors can use active investing to take advantage of short-term trading opportunities - an opportunity to perhaps outperform the market. The potential for higher returns within a short period of time is the main allure of active investing.

ii. Flexibility:

Active Money Managers generally can invest more freely than their passive counterparts as they are not tied to any index. This means that a particular client's ethical or other requirements can be accommodated.

iii. Capital Allocation:

Active investors can strategically allocate capital to sectors or industries they believe will outperform. This ability to make active decisions about where to allocate resources allows for a dynamic approach to portfolio construction.

iv. **Risk Management:**

Active investing enables money managers to adjust investors' portfolios to align with prevailing market conditions. For example, they can minimize potential losses by avoiding certain sectors, regions, etc., in order to reduce their clients' risks in the market.

v. **Tax Management:**

Active money managers can tailor tax management strategies to individual investors. For instance, by selling investments that are losing money to offset the taxes on the big winners.

vi. **Managerial Expertise:**

Many actively managed funds are overseen by professional fund managers with expertise in specific industries or asset classes. Investors benefit from the experience and knowledge of these managers when making investment decisions.

Drawbacks Of Active Investing

Active investing, while offering the potential for higher returns, also comes with several drawbacks. Here are some considerations:

i. Performance Is Dependent On The Skill Of The Manager:

Without a skilled and talented active money manager, there is a risk of investing in an actively managed fund that underperforms. Active managers are free to buy any investment they think would bring high returns, which is great when the analysts are right but terrible when they are wrong.

ii. Takes A Significant Amount Of Time:

Active investing takes time. Much of this time is spent researching the market, combing through dense financial reports to learn more about specific securities, and then acting on that information.

iii. Market Timing Risks:

Attempting to time the market introduces risks. Even skilled investors may struggle to accurately predict short-term market movements, leading to suboptimal investment decisions and potential losses.

iv. <u>**Higher Costs:**</u>

Active investing can be costly due to the potential for numerous transaction costs and high active management fees. Payment is made for the expertise and resources required for active managers, regardless of how successfully the fund performs. All those fees and costs over decades of investing can erode returns.

v. <u>**Minimum Investment Amounts:**</u>

Many active funds and investments often set minimum investment thresholds for prospective investors. For example, a hedge fund might require new investors to make a starting investment of £200,000.

Active investors often use quantitative and technical analysis, including ratio analysis, stock chart analysis and other mathematical measures to determine whether to buy or sell.

Passive Investing

Passive investing is an investment strategy that aims to replicate the performance of a specific market index or benchmark rather than attempting to outperform it. It is an investing style that maximizes returns by minimizing buying and selling. Most people graduate from pre-investor status and enter the investment world through the window of passive investing, which is the most common starting point for beginner investors.

The passive investor type usually employs all the basics of sound personal financial planning. This includes owning your own home, funding tax-deferred retirement plans, implementing asset allocation, and saving at least 10% of earnings, among other principles. If you follow these foundational principles and begin early enough in life, then passive investing is likely all you will ever need to attain financial independence.

The defining characteristic of passive investment strategies is their simplicity, requiring less knowledge and skill, making them accessible to the general populace. "Buy and hold" with mutual funds or stocks, fixed asset allocation, averaging down, and buying real estate at retail prices are examples of passive investment strategies.

Passive investors often use investment vehicles like index funds or exchange-traded funds (ETFs) to gain exposure to a broad market index. These funds hold a diversified portfolio of assets that mirror the components of a specific index. Diversification across a wide range of assets within an index is a significant emphasis of passive investing. This approach helps spread risk and reduces the impact of poorly performing individual securities on the overall portfolio.

Benefits Of Passive Investing

Passive investing offers several benefits that appeal to a wide range of investors. Here are some of the key advantages:

i. **Lower Costs:**

Passive investment strategies, especially those utilizing index funds or ETFs, generally have lower management fees compared to actively managed funds. These lower costs contribute to higher net returns for investors over the long term.

ii. **Diversification:**

Passive investing often involves allocating funds to broad market indexes, providing instant diversification across a wide range of assets. This diversification helps spread risk and reduces the impact of poorly performing individual securities on the overall portfolio.

iii. Market Exposure:

Passive investing allows investors to gain exposure to entire markets or specific segments of the market without the need for in-depth research or individual stock selection. This is particularly beneficial for investors seeking broad market participation.

iv. Simplicity And Accessibility:

Passive investing is straightforward and accessible, making it suitable for both novice and experienced investors. Investors can easily understand and implement a passive strategy without the need for continuous monitoring or complex decision-making.

v. Historical Performance:

Over various time periods, passive strategies, particularly those tracking major market indices, have demonstrated competitive and sometimes superior performance compared to actively managed funds, especially after accounting for fees.

vi. Long-Term Focus:

Passive investing encourages a long-term perspective, aligning with the idea that, over time, markets tend to grow, and short-term fluctuations even out. This approach is well-suited for investors with a patient investment horizon.

Drawbacks Of Passive Investing

While passive investing has numerous benefits, it's important to be aware of its potential drawbacks. Here are some considerations:

i. **Limited Outperformance Potential:**

    Passive investing aims to match the returns of a specific benchmark. As a result, it may miss opportunities to outperform the market, especially during periods when skilled active managers can identify undervalued securities or take advantage of market inefficiencies.

ii. **Inflexibility:**

    Passive portfolios are designed to replicate the composition of a specific index. This can lead to inflexibility, as investors are essentially "locked in" with the securities in the index, regardless of changing market conditions or the fundamentals of individual companies.

iii. <u>Potential For Downside In Bear Markets:</u>

During bear markets, passive investors may experience losses in line with the overall market. Active managers, on the other hand, have the ability to move into defensive positions or assets that may perform better during downturns.

iv. <u>Market Cap Weighting:</u>

Many passive strategies utilize market-capitalization weighting, where larger companies have a greater impact on the index. Consequently, investors in a passive fund may end up with a significant concentration in a few large stocks, potentially increasing risk.

v. <u>Overemphasis On Overvalued Stocks:</u>

Passive investing may lead to an overemphasis on overvalued stocks, as the strategy involves buying stocks in proportion to their market capitalization. This can result in holding stocks that are trading at higher valuations, posing a risk to investors.

26. Dollar-Cost And Pound-Cost Averaging

Dollar-Cost Averaging (DCA) and Pound-Cost Averaging (PCA) essentially embody the same principles, with the terminology varying based on the currency in use. Dollar-Cost Averaging is commonly employed in the United States, where the currency is the US dollar, while Pound-Cost Averaging is a term more frequently associated with the United Kingdom, where the currency is the British pound.

DCA and PCA are investment strategies that involve regularly investing a fixed amount of money into a particular investment, regardless of its current price. By consistently investing the same amount of money each time, you will acquire more of an investment when its price is low and less when its price is high. This strategy "smooths" out the purchase price over time and eliminates much of the detailed work involved in attempting to time the market.

Here's a quick summary of how DCA and PCA works:

i. **Regular Investments**:

    Instead of investing a lump sum of money at once, Investors commit to investing a fixed amount of money at regular intervals, such as monthly, quarterly, or any other consistent period. The same sum goes into the market regardless of asset prices.

ii. Buy More When Prices Are Low:

Since a fixed amount is invested, more units of the investment are automatically bought when prices are lower, and fewer units are bought when prices are higher. Over time, this can mean a lower average cost per share.

iii. Smoothing Out Market Volatility:

By consistently investing over time, DCA and PCA help to smooth out the impact of short-term market fluctuations. It reduces the risk of making poor investment decisions based on short-term market fluctuations by spreading investments over time.

iv. Long-Term Perspective:

DCA and PCA are often associated with a long-term investment horizon. The strategy assumes that, over time, markets tend to trend upward, and short-term market movements become less significant.

Dollar-Cost Averaging and Pound-Cost Averaging are in contrast to attempting to time the market, where an investor tries to buy or sell assets based on predictions of future price movements. This strategy adopts a more disciplined and systematic approach, recognizing the challenge of accurately predicting short-term market movements. The underlying principle emphasizes consistent, periodic investment amounts with the goal of mitigating the impact of market volatility over time.

While Dollar-Cost Averaging and Pound-Cost Averaging can be a sensible strategy for some investors, It is important to note that it doesn't guarantee profits, and the success of the strategy depends on the performance of the underlying investment

.

By making regular investments with the same amount of money each time, you will buy more of an investment when its price is low and less of an investment when its price is high.

27. Long-Term Buy And Hold Investing

Buy and Hold is a long-term investment strategy in which an investor purchases securities (such as stocks, bonds, or real estate) and retains them for an extended period, irrespective of short-term market fluctuations. The fundamental principle behind this strategy is the belief that, over the long term, the market tends to grow, leading to an increase in the value of investments.

Here are some key features of the Buy and Hold strategy:

i. **Long-Term Perspective:**

Investors employing the Buy and Hold strategy typically have a long-term investment horizon, often spanning many years or even decades. The focus is on the overall growth potential of the investments over an extended period rather than short-term price movements.

ii. **Minimization Of Trading Activity:**

Unlike more active trading strategies, Buy and Hold investors generally do not engage in frequent buying and selling of securities. They carefully make their initial investment decisions and then hold onto those investments through various market conditions.

iii.   Riding Out Market Volatility:

Buy and Hold investors are less concerned with short-term market fluctuations. They believe that, over time, the market has historically shown an upward trend, and the impact of short-term volatility is less significant when viewed in the context of long-term investment.

iv.   Income Generation:

In addition to potential capital appreciation, some Buy and Hold investors focus on income generation from their investments. For example, dividend-paying stocks or interest-bearing bonds can provide a steady stream of income over time.

v.   Lower Transaction Costs:

Since Buy and Hold investors do not engage in frequent trading, they may incur lower transaction costs compared to more active trading strategies. This can be advantageous, especially when considering the impact of transaction fees on investment returns.

vi.   Patience And Discipline:

Successful Buy And Hold investing requires patience and discipline. It involves resisting the temptation to react to short-term market fluctuations or news events and maintaining confidence in the long-term potential of the chosen investments.

Buy and hold investing is often associated with a more passive investment style, and it contrasts with active trading strategies that involve frequent buying and selling with the goal of profiting from short-term price movements. While this can be a sound strategy for many investors, it is important to periodically review and rebalance the portfolio to ensure it remains aligned with the investor's financial goals and risk tolerance.

Successful Buy And Hold investing requires patience and discipline. It involves resisting the temptation to react to short-term market fluctuations and maintaining confidence in the long-term potential of the chosen investments.

28. Income Investing

Income investing is an investment strategy focused on generating a steady stream of income from your investment portfolio. Investors employing this strategy seek assets that provide regular cash pay-outs, such as interest or dividends, rather than relying primarily on capital appreciation.

The goal is often to create a consistent and reliable source of income, which can be particularly appealing for investors looking to supplement their current income or fund their retirement. Here are the key principles of income investing:

i. **Above Average Payout:**

It favours assets that pay out above-average dividends. Examples include dividend stocks, bonds, REITs, etc.

ii. **Capital Preservation:**

Preservation of capital is emphasized more than rapid share price appreciation. The focus is on assets producing consistent income, not quick profits from speculation.

iii. **A Conservative Approach To Investing:**

Income investing is generally considered a more conservative approach suited for investors wanting regular cash flow, such as retirees. However, growth investments can still be incorporated.

iv.   Diversification:

Diversifying across income-generating asset classes, market sectors, and geographic regions helps mitigate risk if any single investment underperforms.

v.   Quality Of Asset Selection:

Income investing success depends on selecting high-quality assets with strong fundamentals and steady distributions over chasing the highest yields, which can be risky.

The income received from the portfolio can either be reinvested or used to fund lifestyle needs. Income investing provides a tangible return in the form of cash flows along with modest capital appreciation. For investors wanting an income stream, it can serve as an attractive strategy.

It is important to note that while income investing can provide a reliable cash flow, it is not without risks. Market conditions, interest rate fluctuations, and economic factors can impact the performance of income-generating assets. Investors should carefully assess their financial goals, risk tolerance, and time horizon before adopting an income investing strategy.

29. Value Investing

Value investing is an investment strategy pioneered by Benjamin Graham and David Dodd that involves buying stocks or other financial instruments that are believed to be trading below their intrinsic value. The underlying philosophy of value investing is based on the idea that markets can sometimes misprice assets, presenting opportunities for investors to buy securities at a discount relative to their true worth and generate returns when the market eventually recognizes their worth.

Here are some key principles of value investing:

i. **Intrinsic Value:**

Value investors attempt to estimate the intrinsic or fundamental value of a security. This involves analyzing the financial health of a company, assessing its future cash flows, evaluating its competitive position, and other factors that may affect its true worth.

ii. **Margin Of Safety:**

Value investors seek a margin of safety by purchasing assets at a price significantly below their estimated intrinsic value. This provides a cushion against unforeseen events or errors in valuation, reducing the risk of permanent capital loss.

iii. **Long-Term Perspective:**

Value investing is often associated with a long-term investment horizon. Instead of focusing on short-term market fluctuations, value investors are interested in the long-term growth potential of a fundamentally sound company.

iv. **Contrarian Approach:**

Value investors may take a contrarian approach, meaning they are willing to go against prevailing market sentiments. If a stock is undervalued due to temporary setbacks or negative sentiment, a value investor may see an opportunity to buy at a discount.

v. **Quality Companies:**

Value investors often look for companies with strong fundamentals, such as a history of stable earnings, low debt levels, and a competitive advantage in their industry. They believe that such companies are more likely to weather economic downturns and provide consistent returns over time.

vi. <u>Patient Discipline:</u>

Successful value investing requires patience and discipline. Value investors may need to wait for the market to recognize the true value of their investments, and they are generally not swayed by short-term market noise.

It is important to note that while value investing has been a successful strategy for many investors, it is not without risks. The market may take a long time to recognize the value of a particular investment, and undervalued stocks may remain undervalued or decline further. Additionally, the investment landscape can change, and not all value investments turn out to be profitable. As with any investment strategy, thorough research and an understanding of the associated risks are crucial.

30. Growth Investing

Growth investing is an investment strategy that focuses on investing in stocks or other securities of companies that are expected to grow at an above-average rate compared to other companies. The primary goal of growth investing is to achieve capital appreciation by participating in the potential expansion of a company's earnings, revenue, or other key financial metrics.

Key characteristics of growth investing include:

i. <u>Emphasis On Future Potential:</u>

Growth investors are less concerned with the current valuation metrics and more focused on the future growth prospects of a company. They believe that companies with strong growth potential will see their stock prices rise as the companies expand.

ii. <u>High Price-To-Earnings (P/E) Ratios</u>:

Growth stocks often have higher price-to-earnings (P/E) ratios compared to value stocks. Investors are willing to pay a premium for the growth potential of these companies, even if their current earnings may not justify the high valuation.

iii. Innovation And Technology:

Many growth companies operate in innovative and rapidly evolving industries, such as technology, biotechnology, and other sectors with high growth potential. These companies may be developing new products, services, or technologies that have the potential to disrupt industries and generate substantial returns.

iv. Limited Or No Dividends:

Growth companies may reinvest their earnings back into the business rather than paying dividends. This is because they believe that reinvesting in the company's growth initiatives will yield a higher return for shareholders in the long run.

v. Volatility:

Growth stocks can be more volatile than more established, stable companies. The market's perception of a company's growth potential can lead to significant price swings, and investors in growth stocks may experience both rapid price increases and sharp declines.

vi. Long-Term Horizon:

Growth investing often involves a longer-term perspective. Investors may be willing to hold onto their positions for an extended period, allowing the company's growth story to unfold.

While growth investing can offer substantial returns, it is important to recognize that it also comes with higher risk. Not all high-growth companies succeed, and the potential for significant price volatility means that investors may experience both substantial gains and losses. As with any investment strategy, careful research, diversification, and an understanding of individual risk tolerance are crucial for successful growth investing.

The primary goal of growth investing is to achieve capital appreciation by participating in the potential expansion of a company's earnings, revenue, or other key financial metrics.

31. SRI And ESG Investing

Socially Responsible Investing (SRI) and Environmental, Social, and Governance (ESG) Investing are approaches to investment that take into consideration not only financial returns but also the broader impact of investments on society and the environment.

These investment strategies aim to align investments with ethical values, sustainability principles, or social change objectives. The focus is to seek out investments in companies with strong ethical principles and social responsibility practices, that align with the Investor's values and beliefs.

Key characteristics of SRI and ESG are summarised below:

- They favour companies with positive track records in areas like climate change, human rights, and governance transparency. Companies with poor metrics in these areas of focus get avoided.

- Common investing approaches include positive screening to invest in companies that meet sustainability criteria, negative screening to exclude companies in industries like tobacco, gambling, or weapons manufacturing, and shareholder advocacy to positively influence corporate policies.

- Goals include promoting clean energy, advancing diversity and inclusion, improving community relations, or spurring progression on a variety of environmental issues companies face. The company's impact on the environment, such as its carbon footprint, energy efficiency, and resource use are also considered in the investment selection.

- Investors who prioritize ethical or sustainable considerations in their investment decisions may be willing to accept slightly lower financial returns if it means aligning their portfolios with their values. However, this trade-off is not always clear-cut, and there is growing evidence suggesting that companies with strong environmental, social, and governance practices can, in the long run, perform competitively or even outperform their counterparts.

- The inclusion of SRI and ESG factors in analysis aims to reduce investment risks and tap into growing consumer demand for conscious brands. The investment choice is heavily data-driven and involves the use of specialized ratings and indices to guide investment decisions.

Both Socially Responsible Investing (SRI) and Environmental, Social, and Governance (ESG) investing are gaining popularity as investors increasingly recognize the importance of aligning their financial goals with their values. As the field of SRI and ESG investing continues to evolve, it's likely that there will be increased attention on measuring both financial and non-financial performance to provide a more comprehensive view of investment success.

SRI and ESG Investing are approaches to investment that take into consideration not only financial returns but also the broader impact of investments on society and the environment.

PART 7:

INVESTMENT CHOICES

32. Index Investing

Investing in the stock market can feel like an overwhelming endeavour, but there is a powerful tool at your disposal that can help you achieve your financial goals with simplicity and efficiency: Index Investing. Consider them as your investing superpower, a way to harness the potential of the stock market while minimizing risks and costs.

Index investing is a game-changer for investors of all levels. It involves buying funds (like mutual funds or exchange-traded funds - ETFs) that track a specific market index, such as the S&P 500 or the NASDAQ. Instead of trying to beat the market, the goal is to mirror its performance by holding a diversified portfolio mirroring the components of the chosen index.

This approach has reshaped the way people engage with their financial portfolios, providing a robust alternative to active management. The beauty of this strategy lies in its straightforwardness – a compelling factor for both seasoned investors and those new to the financial landscape.

Let us delve into the essence of this superpower and understand how it can elevate your investment journey.

i. <u>Diversification Magic:</u>

Index investing inherently offers diversification, spreading your investment across a multitude of companies and sectors. This shields your portfolio from the impact of poor-performing individual stocks, providing a more stable and resilient investment foundation.

ii. <u>Cost-Efficiency:</u>

The low fees associated with index funds are a game-changer. Unlike actively managed funds that often charge higher fees for professional management, index funds operate on a passive basis, minimizing costs and putting more money back into your pocket.

iii. <u>Consistent Performance:</u>

While not designed to outperform the market, index investing aims for consistent and reliable performance over the long term. This stability is particularly appealing for investors seeking gradual, sustained growth without the roller-coaster ride associated with more speculative strategies.

iv. <u>Simplicity In Action:</u>

Index investing eliminates the need for constant monitoring and decision-making. This simplicity is not only attractive for those with busy lifestyles but also reduces the stress often associated with more hands-on investment approaches.

v. Access For All:

Index investing democratizes access to the financial markets. Whether you are a seasoned investor or a novice, the ease of entry allows anyone to leverage this superpower and participate in the wealth-building potential of the market.

How to Unleash Your Indexing Superpower

i. Select Your Index:

Choose an index that aligns with your investment goals and risk tolerance. The S&P 500 is popular for its representation of large-cap U.S. stocks, but various indices cater to specific preferences, including international markets, technology, or sustainable investments.

ii. Choose The Right Vehicle:

Invest in index funds or exchange-traded funds (ETFs) that track your chosen index. These funds are readily available through various brokerage platforms, offering flexibility in how you integrate them into your portfolio.

iii. <u>Stay The Course:</u>

Patience is key. Index investing is about the long game. Resist the urge to react to short-term market fluctuations and stay committed to your investment strategy.

In the realm of investing, the superpower of index investing has emerged as a beacon of simplicity, cost-effectiveness, and consistent performance. By embracing this strategy, investors can unlock the door to a more accessible, stress-free, and potentially rewarding financial journey.

The beauty of index investing strategy lies in its straightforwardness – a compelling factor for both seasoned investors and those new to the investing landscape.

33. Individual Stock Investing Vs. Index Investing

The world of investing offers a myriad of options, and two of the most common approaches are individual stock investing and index investing. While both methods provide opportunities for wealth creation, they cater to different investment philosophies, strategies, and risk appetites. Here is a comprehensive look at both approaches, highlighting their advantages and disadvantages.

Individual Stock Investing

Individual stock investing involves selecting specific company stocks to include in your portfolio. It requires research on fundamentals, financials, management, trends, and industry dynamics.

Advantages Of Individual Stock Investing

i. Potential For Outperformance:

Picking individual stocks gives investors the opportunity to outperform the market if they can identify undervalued companies or those with strong growth potential.

ii.   **Customization:**

You have full control over your portfolio, allowing you to tailor it to your investment objectives, risk tolerance, and personal preferences.

iii. **Dividend Income:**

Many individual stocks pay dividends, providing a steady stream of income that can be attractive for income-focused investors.

iv.   **Ownership And Voting Rights:**

Investing in individual stocks gives you a direct stake in a company, which means you may have voting rights and a say in corporate decisions.

v.   **Active Management:**

Some investors enjoy the process of researching and actively managing their portfolios. For those with the time and inclination, individual stock investing can be a rewarding intellectual pursuit.

Individual stock investing involves picking individual company stocks to include in your portfolio.

Disadvantages Of Individual Stock Investing

i.   Higher Risk:

Investing in individual stocks comes with higher risk compared to index investing. A poorly performing company can significantly impact the overall portfolio and achieving diversification can be challenging.

ii.   Time-Consuming:

Successful stock picking requires thorough research and ongoing monitoring. This can be time-consuming and may not be suitable for everyone.

iii.   Expertise Required:

It requires a good understanding of financial markets, company analysis, and economic trends to make informed decisions.

iv.   Volatility:

Individual stocks can be more volatile than diversified index funds, subjecting you to higher market fluctuations.

Index Investing Superpower

We covered the superpowers and advantages of Index Investing in Chapter 32. Index investing is a passive strategy that requires minimal effort. It is an excellent choice for investors who prefer a hands-off approach. Some of its unique benefits are lower costs, diversification, and efficiency. Below are some drawbacks of index investing:

Disadvantages Of Index Investing

i. Average Market Returns:

Index funds aim to match the market, so you won't outperform it. If you are looking for the potential to beat the market, this may not be the best strategy.

ii. No Control Over Components:

You have limited control over the composition of your portfolio when investing in an index. It is a one-size-fits-all approach. If certain stocks perform poorly, they still affect the overall performance of the index.

iii. Market Weighted:

Most indexes are market-cap weighted, meaning larger companies have a greater influence. This could lead to a lack of exposure to smaller, potentially high-growth companies.

iv.   <u>**No Voting Rights:**</u>

When you invest in an index fund, you don't own individual stocks and therefore don't have voting rights in the companies within the index.

Index investing inherently offers diversification, spreading your investment across a multitude of companies and sectors. This shields your portfolio from the impact of poor-performing individual stocks, providing a more stable and resilient investment foundation.

So, Which is Better - Individual Stock Or Indexing?

The choice between individual stock investing and index investing depends on the Investor's financial goals, risk tolerance, time commitment, and expertise. It is crucial to carefully consider your circumstances and investment objectives before deciding on an approach.

Here are some guidelines:

- If you have the time, expertise, and desire to research and manage individual stocks, and you are comfortable with the higher risk and potential for greater returns, an individual stock investing approach may be suitable.

- If you prefer a low-maintenance, diversified, and cost-effective strategy with the aim of steady, market-matching returns, index investing is an excellent choice, especially for long-term investors, index investing may be suitable.

- Many investors find a balanced approach by combining both strategies. They may invest primarily in index funds for stability and diversification while allocating a smaller portion of their portfolio to individual stocks for the potential of outperformance.

Ultimately, your investment strategy should reflect your financial objectives and your comfort with risk and effort. Additionally, seeking advice from financial professionals can be beneficial in making informed decisions.

When trying to get as much return as you can for the least amount of risk, your number one concern should be diversification.

34. UK Stock – FTSEs 100, 250, FTSE All-Share

The United Kingdom (UK) stock market, often referred to as the London Stock Exchange (LSE), is one of the oldest and most prominent stock markets in the world. It plays a vital role in the global financial system and provides a platform for trading various financial instruments such as stocks, bonds, and exchange-traded funds (ETFs).

Key indices that represent the performance of the UK stock market include:

i. **FTSE 100:**

The FTSE 100, often referred to as the "Financial Times Stock Exchange 100 Index", is a stock market index that represents the 100 largest publicly traded companies on the London Stock Exchange (LSE) based on their market capitalization. In other words, it is an index of the 100 largest companies in the UK in terms of market cap. Market capitalization is calculated by multiplying the company's share price by its total number of outstanding shares.

The FTSE 100 is widely followed and used as a benchmark for the performance of the UK stock market. The index is diverse and includes companies from various sectors such as finance, energy, healthcare, consumer goods, and more. This diversity is intended to provide a broad representation of the UK economy. Changes in the composition of the FTSE 100 are periodically made to reflect the evolving stock market landscape.

ii. **FTSE 250:**

The FTSE 250, also known as the "Financial Times Stock Exchange 250 Index", is another stock market index on the London Stock Exchange (LSE). However, it represents the 250 companies with market capitalizations that rank between the 101st and 350th largest on the LSE. These companies are often referred to as mid-cap companies, which are generally smaller in size but still significant players in the UK economy.

The index is diverse, covering a wide range of sectors, including industrials, consumer services, financials, healthcare, and technology. This diversity provides a more comprehensive representation of the UK economy than the FTSE 100, which is more concentrated in larger, often multinational, companies. The FTSE 250 is often considered a barometer of the health of the domestic UK economy. Like the FTSE 100, the composition of the FTSE 250 is reviewed periodically to ensure it remains representative of the market.

iii. **FTSE All-Share Index:**

The FTSE All-Share Index is a broader stock market index that represents the performance of the entire UK equity market. It includes companies from both the FTSE 100 and FTSE 250, as well as small-cap companies. Essentially, it aims to cover about 98% of the market capitalization of all companies listed on the London Stock Exchange (LSE).

Due to its broad coverage, the FTSE All-Share provides a more comprehensive view of the UK equity market compared to the FTSE 100 or FTSE 250 alone. It includes companies from various sectors and industries, offering a diverse representation of the UK economy. Like other FTSE indices, the FTSE All-Share undergoes regular reviews and rebalancing to ensure that it accurately reflects changes in the market. This typically occurs on a quarterly basis.

Investment products such as index funds and exchange-traded funds (ETFs) are available for investors who want to track the performance of the FTSE All-Share. These financial instruments offer exposure to a broad spectrum of UK stocks.

35. US Stock – S&P 500, Dow Jones, NASDAQ

The USA Stock Market, often referred to simply as the U.S. Stock Market, is one of the largest and most influential financial markets in the world. It serves as a vital hub for capital allocation, investment, and the trading of various financial instruments, including stocks, bonds, exchange-traded funds (ETFs), and more.

The U.S. stock market is renowned for its diversity and scale. It is characterized by extensive investor participation, ranging from individual retail investors to institutional investors like mutual funds, pension funds, and hedge funds. This diversity of investors contributes to market liquidity and provides opportunities for a broad spectrum of investment strategies.

Key indices that represent the performance of the U.S. stock market include:

i.   **S&P 500 (Standard & Poor's 500):**

The S&P 500, or Standard & Poor's 500, is one of the most widely followed stock market indices in the world and serves as a benchmark for the overall performance of the U.S. stock market. It is an equity index that tracks the performance of 500 of the largest and most widely traded companies in the United States. These companies are chosen by the index committee at S&P Dow Jones Indices, which selects companies based on various criteria such as market capitalization, liquidity, and industry representation.

The index includes companies from various sectors, such as technology, healthcare, finance, consumer goods, and more. Investors can gain exposure to the S&P 500 through various investment products, including index funds and exchange-traded funds (ETFs). These financial instruments aim to replicate the performance of the index and allow investors to diversify their holdings across a broad array of U.S. stocks.

While the S&P 500 is a U.S. index, its performance is closely watched globally, and it is used as a reference point for assessing global market trends and risk sentiment.

ii. **Dow Jones Industrial Average (DJIA):**

Often referred to simply as the Dow or DJIA, this is one of the oldest stock market indices in the United States. It is a stock market index that measures the performance of 30 large, publicly traded companies listed on stock exchanges in the United States. These companies are considered blue-chip stocks and are leaders in their respective industries.

The index includes companies from various sectors such as technology, healthcare, finance, and consumer goods, providing a broad representation of the U.S. stock market. The value of the Dow is calculated using a price-weighted average, which means that the stocks with higher prices have more influence on the index's value. Changes in the index are often seen as indicators of the overall health and performance of the U.S. stock market.

It is important to note that while the Dow is widely followed, it represents only a small portion of the total U.S. stock market. Other major indices, such as the S&P 500 and the NASDAQ Composite, provide a more comprehensive view of the overall market performance due to their broader scope.

iii.   **NASDAQ:**

The NASDAQ, short for the National Association of Securities Dealers Automated Quotations, is a stock market index that includes a wide range of stocks listed on the NASDAQ stock exchange. It is one of the major stock market indices used to gauge the performance of the broader stock market, particularly in the technology and internet sectors.

The index is market-capitalization-weighted. This means that larger companies, based on their market capitalization (the total market value of their outstanding shares), have a greater impact on the index's value. As a result, the performance of larger technology companies can significantly influence the NASDAQ Composite.

Due to its composition, which includes many high-growth and often more volatile stocks, the NASDAQ Composite can experience significant price swings. It is known for being more volatile compared to other major indices like the Dow Jones or the S&P 500.

It is important to note that there are other NASDAQ indices, such as the NASDAQ 100, which focuses on the 100 largest non-financial companies listed on the NASDAQ. Each index serves different purposes and provides insights into different segments of the market.

The US stock market stands as a symbol of economic vitality, innovation, and opportunity. Its role in the global financial landscape is unrivalled, and it continues to serve as a critical mechanism for companies, investors, and the broader economy.

36. World Stock – MSCI World, FTSE All-World

Understanding the dynamics of the world stock market is important for investors seeking global exposure, diversification, and a comprehensive view of economic trends. It involves considering factors such as currency movements, geopolitical events, and economic indicators that can impact markets on a global scale.

Two common indices that represent the performance of the world stock market are:

i. <u>MSCI World Index:</u>

The MSCI World Index is a widely used benchmark for global equity markets. Maintained by Morgan Stanley Capital International (MSCI), the index is designed to represent the performance of large and mid-cap stocks across 23 developed countries across North America, Europe, Asia, and the Pacific region. It encompasses a broad range of sectors and industries covering approximately 85% of the free float-adjusted market capitalization in each country.

The MSCI World Index is well-diversified, offering exposure to a variety of industries and regions. This diversification is intended to mitigate the impact of poor performance in any single country or sector on the overall index. It serves as a benchmark for many institutional investors, fund managers, and financial professionals to evaluate the performance of their global equity portfolios.

For investors seeking exposure to global equity markets, the MSCI World Index provides a valuable tool. Exchange-traded funds (ETFs) and other investment products are often designed to track the performance of this index, allowing investors to gain broad exposure to developed markets worldwide. The index is typically reported in both U.S. dollars and local currencies, enabling investors to assess performance with and without the impact of currency fluctuations.

ii. **FTSE All-World Index:**

The FTSE All-World Index is a global equity index aiming to represent the performance of large and mid-cap stocks from developed and emerging markets worldwide. It is part of the FTSE Global Equity Index Series, which includes various indices covering different regions and market segments.

Like many major global indices, the FTSE All-World Index is market-capitalization-weighted. This means that the weight of each constituent stock is determined by its market capitalization, giving more significant influence on larger companies. The index is designed to be well-diversified across sectors and regions, providing investors with exposure to a wide range of industries and geographic locations. Diversification aims to reduce the impact of poor performance in any single sector or country on the overall index.

Regular reviews and rebalancing ensure that the FTSE All-World Index accurately reflects the current state of the global equity market. Many institutional investors, fund managers, and financial professionals use it as a benchmark to assess the performance of their global equity portfolios. The index is often reported in both U.S. dollars and local currencies, enabling investors to evaluate performance with and without the impact of currency fluctuations.

Both the MSCI World Index And the FTSE All-World Index provide a comprehensive view of global equity markets, making them valuable tools for investors seeking broad exposure to both developed and emerging markets.

PART 8:

EMOTIONS AND INVESTING PITFALLS TO AVOID

---

37. Handling Emotions When Investing

Investing is often likened to an emotional rollercoaster. Major market swings, economic uncertainty, and geopolitical events can evoke a range of emotions from anxiety to thrill-seeking excitement. However, allowing emotions to dictate financial decisions can prove costly.

Extreme market highs may tempt investors to impulsively purchase assets, while severe lows can trigger panic selling - both actions that can detract from overall returns. Every investor experience emotive impulse but mastering the ability to keep emotions in check is crucial. In this chapter, we will explore the most common emotions investors experience and strategies to handle them effectively.

i.   Fear:

Fear is a natural response to uncertainty and potential losses, often arising during market downturns or economic crises. Investors fear losing their hard-earned money, which can lead to panic selling and missed opportunities for recovery.

ii.   Greed:

Greed is the desire for excessive wealth or returns, leading investors to take on too much risk in pursuit of higher profits. It can manifest when markets are surging, and investors see others making substantial gains. Greed may result in risky investment decisions, overconfidence, and chasing high returns without considering risks.

iii. **Anxiety And Stress:**

Anxiety and stress can result from the uncertainty of investing, especially for those new to the market. These emotions can become overwhelming, impacting decision-making.

iv. **Regret:**

Investors may experience regret when making a losing trade or missing out on a lucrative investment. This emotion can lead to second-guessing and impulsive actions to rectify perceived mistakes.

v. **Frustration:**

Frustration can occur when the market doesn't behave as expected or when investments underperform. Managing frustration is crucial to avoid making emotional decisions.

vi.   <u>Regret</u>:

Investors may experience regret when they make a losing trade or miss out on a lucrative investment. This emotion can lead to second-guessing and impulsive actions to rectify perceived mistakes.

vii.   <u>Impatience</u>:

Impatience may arise when investors expect overnight success rather than long-horizon growth. This emotion can prompt rapid strategy switches as investors seek quick results.

viii.   <u>Overconfidence:</u>

Overconfidence occurs when investors believe their ability to predict market movements or pick winning stocks is greater than it actually is. This can lead to the misconception of having unique insights or abilities, resulting in excessive risks without proper research or diversification.

These emotive influences can lead to biased thinking, reckless decisions and poor investment discipline if not kept in check through awareness and intentionality. Understanding common pitfalls is the first step to overcoming them.

Strategies For Handling Emotions When Investing

Managing emotions when investing is crucial for successful and rational decision-making. Here are some strategies to help you manage emotions effectively:

i. Educate Yourself:

Knowledge is a powerful tool for calming emotional reactions. Understanding the basics of investing, the market, and the specific assets in your portfolio can provide a sense of control and confidence. The more you understand about the investment markets, the less likely you are to make decisions based on fear or misinformation.

ii. Set Clear Goals:

Establishing clear investment goals and understanding your risk tolerance helps you make informed decisions. Knowing what you are investing for and how much risk you are willing to take can provide a framework for rational decision-making. Having a well-defined plan can help you stay focused during turbulent times.

iii. <u>Diversify Your Portfolio:</u>

Diversification can help spread risk across different assets and reduce the impact of poor performance in any single investment. A well-diversified portfolio can be less susceptible to emotional reactions to short-term market fluctuations.

iv. <u>Have A Long-Term Perspective:</u>

Markets can be volatile in the short term, but historical data shows that they tend to trend upward over the long term. Adopting a long-term perspective can help you ride out short-term fluctuations without succumbing to panic or greed.

v. <u>Create An Investment Plan:</u>

Develop a well-thought-out investment plan that aligns with your goals and risk tolerance. Having a plan in place provides a roadmap for your investments and can help prevent impulsive decisions based on short-term market movements.

vi. <u>Automate Investments:</u>

Set up automatic contributions to your investment accounts. Automation can take emotion out of the equation by ensuring consistent contributions regardless of market conditions. This strategy is particularly effective for long-term, systematic investing.

vii. **Stay Informed, But Avoid Overreacting:**

Stay informed about market developments, economic indicators, and news that may affect your investments. However, avoid making decisions solely based on short-term news or market fluctuations. Emphasize the long-term trends and fundamentals of your investments.

viii. **Practice Mindfulness And Emotional Awareness:**

Be mindful of your emotions and recognize when they might be influencing your decisions. Take a step back, evaluate your investment thesis, and consider the long-term implications before making any major changes.

ix. **Seek Professional Advice:**

If you find it challenging to manage your emotions, consider seeking advice from a financial advisor. They can provide a rational perspective, help you stay focused on your long-term goals, and guide you through market volatility.

Emotions are integral to investing, yet they can be managed to facilitate rational, informed decisions. Understanding common emotional triggers and implementing strategies to handle them allows you to navigate the ups and downs of financial markets with greater confidence and discipline. It is essential to remember that successful investing often involves a balance of rational analysis and emotional resilience.

Understanding common emotional triggers and implementing strategies to handle them allows you to navigate the ups and downs of financial markets with greater confidence and discipline.

38. Pitfalls And Mistakes To Avoid When Investing

Many hesitate to invest due to the fear of financial loss. Fear emerges as the most significant adversary in investing. The fear of losing money not only deters people from trying but also triggers panic selling, leading to the forfeiture of future returns. When combined with the fear of missing out (FOMO), which drives individuals to act greedily or impulsively, fear becomes a dangerous two-headed beast capable of causing harm in both directions.

Even experienced investors sometimes grapple with investment fears; many have made numerous mistakes and endured financial regrets. People often make poor decisions, get carried away by emotions, and experience financial losses due to situations beyond their control. Nevertheless, it is possible to overcome investment fears and adversity.

I've listed a few pitfalls and mistakes to avoid if you aim to be a successful investor and engage in secure investing.

i. Not Investing At All:

The most significant mistake anyone can make is failing to invest at all. Cash is a depreciating asset due to inflation, which erodes its value over time. Investing in assets such as equities, bonds, and commercial properties has proven to be the best way to grow and protect capital from inflation over the long term.

Anyone not investing is missing out tremendously. Early contributions are most valuable as they have the longest time to compound. The best time to invest was YESTERDAY; the next best time is TODAY. Do not delay. Start investing NOW!

ii. <u>Not Having A Plan:</u>

Investing without a clear plan is a recipe for trouble. Planning is an important step in the investing process. Diving straight into investing without a defined plan is one of the biggest mistakes made by investors.

Before embarking on your investing journey, make sure you have answers to these three questions:

- Why am I investing?
- How long am I investing for?
- What is my attitude to risk?

iii. <u>Investing In What You Don't Understand:</u>

Overestimating your abilities and knowledge is a recipe for disaster. You don't know everything; invest in what you understand. Study what you can learn and stick to it. If you don't understand something, don't blindly try it out. You must learn before you can earn. Every investment you make in yourself will pay you dividends for a lifetime.

Invest in what you know and remember the first rule of investing is not to lose money. The more you know about investing, the fewer mistakes you will likely make, and the better your investment performance will be. So, invest in your financial education; it will pay you dividends for a lifetime.

iv. <u>Lack Of Diversification:</u>

Putting all your money into a single investment or asset class exposes you to significant risk. By diversifying, you avoid investing aggressively in one class. The first part of a diversification strategy consists of mixing asset classes by holding various stocks, bonds, cash, real estate, etc.

The second part of a properly diversified portfolio is mixing within asset classes. Opting for a good mix of small-cap, large-cap, international, and industry sector-diverse equities is wise. While a market decline may affect a certain stock or sector, a gain in another might offset the loss. Diversification must never be ignored when investing.

v. <u>Falling For Investment Scams:</u>

Investing is not a get-rich-quick scheme. It doesn't make you rich overnight; it takes decades to accumulate wealth. While the allure of big wins is tempting, victory typically favours steady and patient investors.

Be cautious of investment opportunities that seem too good to be true. Scams and fraudulent schemes abound in the financial world, so conduct due diligence and be sceptical of promises that appear unrealistic.

vi. <u>Ignoring Fees And Costs:</u>

High management fees, brokerage costs, and taxes can erode your returns. The more you pay in fees and associated investing costs, the less of your returns you get to keep. It is essential to be aware of all expenses associated with your investments and seek cost-effective options. If you are using a high-commission fund manager and investing in something with high transaction charges, you are very likely to incur losses.

vii. <u>Short-Term Focus:</u>

Investing with a short-term mindset can lead to missed opportunities and increased risk. Have a long-term perspective and resist the urge to react to short-term market fluctuations. Trying to time the market or chasing quick, speculative gains often leads to losses. Focusing on long-term, sound investment strategies is usually more effective.

viii. **Attempting To Time The Market:**

Market timing is the act of moving investment money in or out of a financial market or switching funds between asset classes based on predictive methods. Trying to time the market by predicting short-term movements is challenging and often leads to poor outcomes. Focus on long-term trends and your investment strategy rather than attempting to predict short-term fluctuations.

ix. **Stock Picking:**

Randomly buying individual stocks of companies that are making headlines due to a recent high-profile IPO is rarely a good idea. By all means, you can allocate a small percentage of your budget to stock-picking ideas if that is your preference. However, stock picking should not form the foundation of your long-term investment strategy.

Beginner investors are better off considering index funds and mutual funds, which comprise hundreds of different companies from around the world within a single fund. With these funds, you won't have to worry about individual stocks bouncing back during market dips. You also won't have to worry about finding the 'right' companies because you own a share of them all from the start. Index and mutual funds allow you to enjoy market-matching returns with minimal effort and near-zero cost.

x.   Following The Herd:

Blindly following the crowd or investing in a particular asset just because it is popular can lead to overvaluation and eventual losses. Make investment choices based on your financial goals and research, not market trends.

Avoiding these investing pitfalls requires a disciplined and informed approach to investing. It is essential to have a well-thought-out investment strategy, adhere to your financial goals, and continuously educate yourself about the financial markets. Making money is more enjoyable than losing it, and steering clear of just one of these investment mistakes can literally make the difference between wealth and poverty.

PART 9:

INVESTING ILLUSTRATIONS

---

39.   Vanguard Brokerage Account

Opening a brokerage investing account with Vanguard involves a series of quick and easy steps. You will need your National Insurance number (UK), your Social Security number (US), debit card details (for a single payment), and/or bank or building society details (if you are planning on setting up a regular savings plan). Here are general steps you might follow:

i.   **Visit the Vanguard Website:**
     Go to the official Vanguard UK website at www.vanguardinvestor.co.uk/ or www.vanguard.com for non-UK residents.

ii. **Select the Account Type:**

     Vanguard offers various types of accounts, including Individual Savings Accounts (ISAs), Stocks and Shares ISA, Self-Invested Personal Pensions (SIPPs), and general investment accounts. Choose the account type that suits your needs.

iii. **Start the Application:**

     Look for a "Sign Up" or "Open an Account" button to begin the application process.

iv.   <u>Complete the Application:</u>

Fill out the required forms and provide the requested personal, financial, and employment information.

v.   <u>Fund your Account:</u>

Deposit funds into your Vanguard account. Vanguard offers different methods for funding your account, such as bank transfers or direct debits.

vi.   <u>Choose Investments:</u>

Select the specific investments you want to purchase. Vanguard offers a range of funds and ETFs. You can also invest in individual stocks if that is your preference.

vii.   <u>Review and Confirm:</u>

Double-check all the information you've entered and the investment choices you've made to ensure accuracy and alignment with your financial goals.

viii.   <u>Submit the Application:</u>

Submit your application for review. You may need to electronically sign certain documents or provide paper forms, depending on Vanguard's requirements.

ix. <u>Wait for Approval:</u>

After submitting your application, Vanguard will review it, and once approved, your account will be activated.

x. <u>Access your Account:</u>

Once your account is open, you can access it online through Vanguard's platform. From there, you can manage your investments, execute trades, and monitor your portfolio.

Keep in mind that specific requirements and processes may change, so it is a good idea to visit the Vanguard website or contact their customer support for the most current and accurate information.

Additionally, in the UK, it's crucial to be aware of tax implications and rules associated with the type of account you are opening (e.g., ISAs, SIPPs), as they may offer tax advantages and come with certain restrictions. It is advisable to consult with a financial advisor or tax professional to make informed decisions based on your specific financial situation and goals.

40. Fidelity Brokerage Account

Opening an Investing account with Fidelity involves a series of quick and easy steps. To get started, you will need your National Insurance number (UK), your Social Security number (US), debit card details (for a single payment), and/or bank or building society details (if you plan on setting up a regular savings plan). Here are the general steps you might follow:

i.   Visit the Fidelity Website:

Go to the official Fidelity website at www.fidelity.co.uk for UK residents or www.fidelity.com for non-UK residents.

ii.   Navigate to the "Open an Account" Section:

Look for a section on the website related to opening an account. This is under "Open an Account" or a similar heading.

iii.   Choose the Type of Account:

Fidelity offers various types of accounts, such as individual brokerage accounts, retirement accounts (like IRAs and SIPPs), and education savings accounts. Select the type of account that suits your investment goals.

iv.   **Provide Personal Information:**

You will need to provide personal information, including your name, address, date of birth, National Insurance or Social Security number, employment information, and financial details.

v.   **Agree to Terms and Conditions:**

Read and agree to the terms and conditions associated with opening an account. Ensure that you understand the fees, commissions, and other relevant details.

vi.   **Choose Account Features:**

Select any additional features or options you want for your account. For example, you may choose to enable margin trading or options trading.

vii.   **Set Up Funding:**

Decide how you will fund your account. You may be able to transfer funds electronically from your bank account, mail a check, or transfer assets from another brokerage.

viii.   **Review Information:**

Carefully review all the information you have provided to ensure accuracy.

ix. **<u>Submit Documentation:</u>**

You may need to submit additional documentation to verify your identity. This could include a copy of your driver's license, a utility bill, or other proof of address.

x. **<u>Wait for Approval:</u>**

After submitting your application, you will need to wait for Fidelity to review and approve your account. This process can take a few days.

xi. **<u>Access your Account:</u>**

Once your account is approved, you should receive information on how to access your online account. This may include setting up a username and password.

xii. **<u>Start Investing:</u>**

Once your account is set up and funded, you can start investing. Fidelity provides various tools and resources to help you make informed investment decisions.

Remember, these steps are a general guide, and the specific process may vary. Always refer to the latest information available on the Fidelity website for the most accurate and up-to-date instructions.

41. Hargreaves Lansdown Brokerage Account

Hargreaves Lansdown is a UK-based investment platform. To open an investing account with Hargreaves Lansdown, follow these general steps:

i. **Visit the Hargreaves Lansdown Website:**

    Go to the official Hargreaves Lansdown website at www.hl.co.uk.

ii. **Navigate to the Account Opening Section:**

    Look for a section on the website related to opening an account. This might be under "Open an Account" or a similar heading.

iii. **Choose the Type of Account:**

    Hargreaves Lansdown offers various types of accounts, including ISAs (Individual Savings Accounts), SIPP (Self-Invested Personal Pension), and general investment accounts. Select the type of account that aligns with your investment goals.

iv. **Provide Personal Information:**

Supply personal information, including your name, address, date of birth, National Insurance number, and other relevant details.

v. **Agree to Terms and Conditions:**

Read and agree to the terms and conditions associated with opening an account. Ensure you understand the fees, commissions, and other relevant details.

vi. **Choose Account Features:**

Select any additional features or options you want for your account. For example, if you are opening a SIPP, you may need to choose investment options within the pension account.

vii. **Set Up Funding:**

Decide how you will fund your account. This may involve transferring funds electronically from your bank account.

viii. **Review Information:**

Carefully review all the information you've provided to ensure accuracy.

ix.   **<u>Submit Documentation:</u>**

You may need to submit additional documentation to verify your identity. This could include a copy of your passport, utility bill, or other proof of address.

x.   **<u>Wait for Approval</u>**:

After submitting your application, you will need to wait for Hargreaves Lansdown to review and approve your account. This process can take a few days.

xi.   **<u>Access your Account:</u>**

Once your account is approved, you should receive information on how to access your online account. This may include setting up a username and password.

xii.   **<u>Start Investing:</u>**

Once your account is set up and funded, you can begin investing. Hargreaves Lansdown provides various tools and resources to help you make informed investment decisions.

Remember, these steps are a general guide, and the specific process may vary. Always refer to the latest information on Hargreaves Lansdown's website or contact their customer service for the most accurate and current details.

42. AJ Bell Brokerage Account

AJ Bell is a UK-based investment platform. You can open an investing account online in minutes. Here are general steps you might follow to open an investing account with AJ Bell:

i.   Visit the AJ Bell Website:

Go to the official AJ Bell website at www.ajbell.co.uk.

ii.   Navigate to the Account Opening Section:

Look for a section on the website related to opening an account. This might be under "Open an Account" or a similar heading.

iii. Choose the Type of Account:

AJ Bell offers various types of accounts, including ISAs (Individual Savings Accounts), SIPP (Self-Invested Personal Pension), and general investment accounts. Select the type of account that aligns with your investment goals.

iv.   Provide Personal Information:

You will need to provide personal information, including your name, address, date of birth, National Insurance number, and other relevant details.

v.   <u>**Agree to Terms and Conditions:**</u>

Read and agree to the terms and conditions associated with opening an account. Make sure you understand the fees, commissions, and other relevant details.

vi.   <u>**Choose Account Features:**</u>

Select any additional features or options you want for your account. For example, if you are opening a SIPP, you may need to choose investment options within the pension account.

vii.   <u>**Set Up Funding:**</u>

Decide how you will fund your account. This may involve transferring funds electronically from your bank account.

viii.   <u>**Review Information:**</u>

Carefully review all the information you've provided to ensure accuracy.

ix.   <u>**Submit Documentation:**</u>

You may need to submit additional documentation to verify your identity. This could include a copy of your passport, utility bill, or other proof of address.

x.   <u>**Wait for Approval:**</u>

After submitting your application, you'll need to wait for AJ Bell to review and approve your account. This process can take a few hours to a few days.

xi.   <u>**Access your Account:**</u>

Once your account is approved, you should receive information on how to access your online account. This may include setting up a username and password.

xii.   <u>**Start Investing:**</u>

Once your account is set up and funded, you can start investing and building your investment portfolio. AJ Bell provides various tools and resources to help you make informed investment decisions.

Remember, these steps are a general guide, and the specific process may vary. Always refer to the latest information on AJ Bell's website or contact their customer service for the most accurate and current details. Happy investing!

IN CLOSING

Congratulations! You've reached the end of this book, and I trust you've gained valuable insights into stock market investing. Grasping the workings of money and securing your finances are among the most crucial skills for a fulfilling life. You don't need to be a genius to achieve financial success; all it takes is a solid understanding of the basics, a well-thought-out plan and strategy, and the commitment to stick with it.

You don't need to know everything from day one to begin investing in the stock market. Every successful investor I know begins with the basics, and many of them started small, gradually building their wealth over time. Regardless of how much or little money you have, the crucial thing is to educate yourself on the fundamentals of how you can make your money work for you. These basics are covered in this book.

I often ask people to tell me their 'WHY' for investing. It's important to know the motivation behind your decision to invest your money. It's okay if you have many answers to this question, but there is a big problem if you have no answer at all. Don't invest based on my recommendation, peer pressure, or FOMO (Fear Of Missing Out). Having clear and defined reasons or purposes for investing is pivotal to achieving success in your investment journey.

I usually conclude my books by emphasizing the significance of financial education. If this is the first book on personal finance and investing you've ever read, don't let it be the last. Explore more books on money management, continue learning, listen to podcasts, ask questions, attend financial literacy seminars, enrol in finance courses, seek knowledge, and make learning a habit. Your financial education is a journey, and continuous learning is the key to long-term financial success.

Commit to learning at least one new thing about money management every day, no matter how small. Stay mindful of your ongoing financial education. Set a specific goal each day or focus on a particular area of personal finance you want to develop. By embracing the mindset that learning is a continuous process, you'll effortlessly advance your education and make significant strides toward achieving the financial freedom and independence you desire!

ABOUT OYENIKE ADETOYE

 Oyenike (also known as Nike) is an impactful speaker, author, and personal finance expert. A Chartered Management Accountant by profession, Nike founded LifTED Finance Consulting Ltd, a private financial firm that educates, coaches, and supports people on their journey through financial fitness and wealth management.

Nike defines success by the number of lives impacted, changed, and empowered through her message of hope in the area of personal finance. Her book series on personal finance and money management provides simple guiding principles that empower people to win with their money. In addition to her professional success, she is happily married and blessed with two beautiful children.

Connect with Oyenike online:

W▶ http://www.liftedfinance.com/

E▶ info@liftedfinance.com

T▶ https://twitter.com/FinanceLifted

F▶ https://www.facebook.com/liftedfinanceconsultingltd/

I ▶ https://www.instagram.com/liftedfinance/

L▶ https://www.linkedin.com/company/liftedfinanceconsulting/

STOCK MARKET INVESTING

BY: OYENIKE ADETOYE ACMA, CGMA

"Successful investing is not about timing the market perfectly; it's about making informed decisions, maintaining discipline, and always learning."

— Oyenike Adetoye

Printed in Great Britain
by Amazon

41583934R00136